T0117104

Why Men Fear Marriage

Why Men Fear Marriage

The Surprising Truth Behind
Why So Many Men Can't Commit

RM JOHNSON

POCKET BOOKS   KAREN HUNTER PUBLISHING

New York   London   Toronto   Sydney

Pocket Books
A Division of Simon & Schuster, Inc.
1230 Avenue of the Americas
New York, NY 10020

Karen Hunter Publishing
A Division of Suitt-Hunter Enterprises, LLC
598 Broadway, 3rd Floor
New York, NY 10012

First Karen Hunter Publishing/Pocket Books trade paperback edition January 2011

POCKET and colophon are registered trademarks of Simon & Schuster, Inc.

For information about special discounts for bulk purchases, please contact Simon & Schuster Special Sales at 1-866-506-1949 or business@simonandschuster.com.

The Simon & Schuster Speakers Bureau can bring authors to your live event. For more information or to book an event contact the Simon & Schuster Speakers Bureau at 1-866-248-3049 or visit our website at www.simonspeakers.com.

Manufactured in the United States of America

10 9 8 7 6 5 4 3 2 1

Library of Congress Cataloging-in-Publication Data is available for the hardcover edition.

ISBN 978-1-4391-0149-0
ISBN 978-1-4391-0150-6 (pbk)
ISBN 978-1-4391-6360-3 (ebook)

To the women who have loved and cared for us
We are thankful

CONTENTS

Contents

Contents

Contents

Contents

Why Men Fear Marriage

INTRODUCTION

Why Men Finally Seek Marriage

If you're thumbing through the pages of this book, I can assume that, whether you're married or not, you have some interest in discovering why men fear marriage. Maybe you have this interest because you would like to marry one day, and after all the dates you've been on, all the relationships you've had, you haven't once come close to receiving that proposal. Or after being divorced once or twice, you're ready to try marriage again. Or maybe it's because all of your girlfriends—women you believe are beautiful, intelligent, and successful—always remark how men today just don't seem to want marriage.

Whatever the reason, I am confident this book will tell you all you need to know to answer the question of why men do indeed fear marriage.

But what I'd like to do before I continue with this introduction is give you a little piece of advice if you happen to be one of the so-called lucky women who are in a relationship that seriously seems to be heading toward marriage.

If you plan on marrying your man and he is under thirty years old—don't! He's too young.

I'm not saying that he's immature, or that he's not smart or successful, or that he doesn't have the most respectable intentions. He's just too young.

If you're at the age, where, on average, you're dating men under the age of thirty, this might be one of the reasons why you're not married. Your man is too busy dating *other* women. It's a conquest of ours that started not long after the first time we had sex.

Young men love the hunt, the chase, the challenge of finding an attractive woman, getting in her head, and talking her into what he wants most. Sex.

For so much of our young lives, this is how we measured success: how many women we have slept with. This is what drives most of us under the age of thirty, and what we think about while at work—what bar or club we're going to go to in order to talk to women.

But don't despair. There's a point when this becomes old to us. The age varies, but it's somewhere around the mid-thirties when one day, we're attempting to have sex with any woman who will allow us to, and the next, we're looking for a wife.

I see it happening to all my friends. They're changing right in front of my eyes. Let me tell you why that is.

Sex is great. You've probably heard this from a male friend of yours, but what men think is even better than sex is new sex.

But there's a point when even new sex becomes the same old thing.

I was speaking to a close friend of mine the other day. He said, "I know I'm sounding like a chick, but I'm tired of having sex if there's no emotional involvement."

I agreed with him, jokingly told him that he did sound like a chick, but I understood exactly where he was coming from.

For the average guy, who has been having sex for almost twenty years, or even more, how much more does he need? What more can we experience that we haven't already felt, or tasted?

But there's something else. We become tired.

You ask, tired of what? From the day-to-day juggling of women.

Most of us, over the course of our dating lives, don't date just one woman at a time. We date three or four or five.

It's wrong, I know. All men know this, but we do it anyway, feeling as though we have to supplement one woman with the next, in order to attain all the qualities we want, but can't find in a single woman.

This is fun for us when we're twenty, or even thirty, but after fifteen or twenty years of dating several women, lying to others, having to schedule your comings and goings so as not to have you bumping into our other women when leaving our houses—this becomes simply exhausting.

Bottom line, we not only get tired of all the calculating, we get tired of you, of having to be a caring, concerned full-time boyfriend five times over. It's hard enough maintaining one relationship.

There will always be a certain amount of drama attached to each partner. We accept that, as I'm sure you do when dating us. But imagine getting drama multiplied by five. Dealing with PMS from five separate women, especially when two or three of your periods occur around the same time.

Imagine buying birthday gifts for five different women, and eating Thanksgiving dinner five separate times. Then there's five Christmas gifts to purchase, five invitations to spend that holiday with your family, not to mention New Year's Eve—11:59 P.M. on December 31 happens only once a year. We have to decide which one of you to spend that moment with.

After so many years, we mature, and determine that we don't feel like dealing with that drama anymore.

Also, over those years of maturation, while we're maxing out our credit cards, buying those Christmas gifts, the smart man, the kind of man you're looking for now, was also going to school, getting an education. He was climbing the corporate ladder, earning and saving money, and acquiring assets, like a home and investments.

So one day, we look around and realize we no longer want to stay out till one A.M. on a Wednesday night and then stagger home, only to wake up with a pounding headache and have to go to work. We want to build on the success we've had on our jobs; we want to climb even higher up that ladder. But once that happens, we don't want to discover that the only person we have to share those accomplishments with is the girl with the beautiful body we met in the club a week ago, took home, had sex with, then woke up to find she had scurried away after vomiting in our sheets.

No, that's not what we want.

When we were kids, after we came home from school with a star on our papers to show our mothers, she rewarded us with a hug and a kiss. We want that again. We want someone who'll appreciate what we've done, what we're doing, and show us that appreciation, that supportive affection.

Around the mid-thirties is when men just naturally settle, when we (most of us, not all of us) get tired of having our guy friends over at all times of night, playing Xbox 360. This is the time when we know we should be eating healthier, and for some reason (whether it's true or not) believe that a woman would make sure that happens.

And as we continue to age, something else happens: we become more aware of our own mortality.

When I was twenty-eight, I told my oldest brother I would never have children.

He lay back on his sofa, crossed his arms under his head, and smiled. "You say that now, but one day you're gonna want a little you in this world."

He was right.

As we near or pass thirty-five, if we haven't already had children, some of us realize that we're about halfway done with our lives, and we ask ourselves, what do we have to show for it? Hmmm, we ponder. A string of women we had sex with, some of them we lied to, led on for years, then finally dumped when they thought we were going to propose.

As mature men, that's no longer enough for us.

These days, whenever I speak with my male friends, the conversations always seem to be about the opposite sex, about the possibility of getting married and having children.

"By this time next year, I'm gonna be married," my friend told me two months ago.

I asked him, to whom? He said he didn't know. He hadn't met her yet. "But it doesn't matter. I'm going to find her, and marry her," he assured me.

That is how serious we become.

Not to say that a man's fear all of a sudden disappears. We're still fearful. But after so many years of meaningless, go-nowhere relationships, we come to understand that our situations are dire.

I watched one forty-year-old friend of mine eat two bowls of Fruity Pebbles for dinner the other night.

After he poured the second bowl, he shook the box, weighing its contents in his hand, and said, "There should be enough left for breakfast tomorrow, and maybe even dinner."

I'll admit that I've eaten cans of tuna for breakfast, a meatless microwaved chicken patty for lunch, pancakes and spinach salad for dinner. And this was not even a year ago. That's not cool. Not . . . cool.

After so many years of doing this, we understand this is not the way we are supposed to live our lives. This is not the way we *want* to live our lives.

Then why don't men just get serious, buckle down, man up, find a woman to love, and get married?

Because, as this book will explain, there are some fears that, as men, we contend with.

We may tell ourselves that we want to find a good woman to date, that we won't even mind if she has children by another man, but then we might start to doubt if her children will like us, wonder what issues we may have to deal with regarding that child's father, and if, for some reason, in the future, the mother has to choose a side, will it be that of the child, the father, or ours?

As men, we often tell ourselves that we are willing to accept a woman exactly as she is, but then we become concerned about the possibility of her changing after we marry her. Will she become a different woman? Will we receive as much sex? Will she gain weight? Will she be unfaithful, divorce us, take the house, our children, and half of everything we own?

But what drives us away from the thought of marriage is not just what we believe might happen, but what we hear, what we've seen with our own eyes as children growing up.

When a man hears from another man—his coworker, best friend, brother, or even father—that marriage is not as enjoyable as it's made out to be, that a man is maybe better off never marrying, we take heed of that warning.

Or when, as children, we see firsthand our own parents' marriage dissolve, we question whether we can make it work when they could not.

These are just a few of the obstacles men face when we contemplate marriage. So with all this to scare us half to death, why would we even think about taking a chance on marriage?

Because, like I said before, men want marriage. We're just a little afraid, and we need just a little help from you.

So, within the pages that follow is not just the information you need to understand why men fear marriage, but advice on what you can do to help that hesitant man through his fear. But before that, chapter 2 will inform you of exactly what types of men are out there, which ones to choose, and which ones to avoid. It'll also give tips on how to approach those men, whether he should take your number or you should take his, and the best way to enjoy the first date.

Beyond that, this book gives you the real reason why some men will date a woman for five or ten years and never marry her, only to turn around and marry the next woman he dates, whom he's known for only six months.

And for you women who are serious about wanting marriage,

and wanting it now, chapter 9 will list the ten steps that will make him say, "Will you marry me?"

Not all men want marriage, but I strongly believe most do. Unfortunately, we hold back from energetically and faithfully pursuing that goal because of our fear of what the outcome might be.

After reading *Why Men Fear Marriage*, I know that you will not just have a better understanding of what has men clinging to their single status, but this book will educate you, help you determine if your man is truly worth considering for marriage, or if you should walk away from him now. It will empower you to see situations the way we, as men, see them, and inform you as to whether he plans to spend the rest of his life with you, or if he's just using you as a "bridge woman." (More on that in chapter 8.)

So, whether you're actively seeking marriage or just want insight into what may present challenges to you when you do decide to look, I am confident that *Why Men Fear Marriage* should help in your search to find answers to all your questions.

Thanks. Now, learn and enjoy.

CHAPTER ONE

Why Men Develop a Negative Opinion toward Marriage

The marriage model

Our parents' marriage, for us, is supposed to be *the* example of what a good marriage is, right? When we watch our mother and father, how they relate as a married couple, this is supposed to be the blueprint for how we're supposed to behave when we grow old enough to marry.

That is the way it's supposed to work, and believe it or not, it does work that way.

Think about your close friends whose parents are still married. Are those friends married now? Many of them probably are.

Now think about your close friends whose parents are divorced, or who were raised by a single parent. How many of them are married today? Most likely not as many.

As kids, if we see that the two people raising us, a mother and father who are in love, get along, treasure their time together, and are happy, we will one day want the same for ourselves.

If we had a happy childhood, one that we knew was created and supervised by our parents, we know we have them to thank for that, and we will look forward to the opportunity to one day give our children the same.

What is interesting is that as children, we don't always have to be happy to later want marriage. Once we are old enough, we understand that it's natural that our parents weren't happy twenty-four hours of the day, either.

Here is where the model is important.

Parents are going to argue. There are going to be disagreements.

My parents are divorced. That happened when I was eight years old.

Building up to that point, they argued a lot. They experienced conflicts they could not resolve. There was a lot of tension between the two of them, which ultimately led to divorce.

Because of their arguing, and their subsequent separation, the message I took away from the experience was, if I get married, and if problems occur, the way to resolve them is to leave. But in doing that, I'd know that the same way my father hurt me with his departure, I will hurt my children. So to avoid that from happening, I told myself that it might be best if I never marry.

But what about the parents who argued but never got divorced? The parents who disagreed and raised their voices sometimes, but then calmed down, talked things out, and resolved their issues? What do the children of those couples believe?

They understand that arguing and the occasional spat is part of marriage, or any worthwhile relationship. But what they also learn is that compromise and understanding is part of that as well. They learned this from hearing the arguments their parents waged, then seeing them resolve those problems. They've seen what years of determination and dedication to a marriage can bring, as opposed to what so many other men see—the failure of their parents' marriage, then their mother and father walking along separate paths, many of them dating for the rest of their lives, but never marrying again.

Guess what kind of effect that has on the average man? How many of us do you believe would be rushing to the altar to find ourselves in the exact same situation as our fathers? That is, even if we knew our fathers.

No father in the home

I don't believe people appreciate just how important fathers are. I often say, if there was no father, there would be no Tiger Woods, just some guy named Eldrick Woods. That's not to say he wouldn't have been a great banker, or cable technician, or Walmart associate. I'm just giving an example of how much influence a father can have on his son's life.

Keeping with Tiger Woods for a moment, he married before he was even thirty years old. That goes against most of what I say in this book. But, then again, I'm speaking from the point of view of a boy who grew up without a father.

Tiger Woods's father was around. He was married to Tiger Woods's mother, and he was present in his son's life.

I imagine that, as a child, just about every morning when Tiger Woods sat himself at the breakfast table, he'd see his parents there. And just about every day, he'd see them interact. But what also happened is what happens with all the other little girls and boys whose fathers are in the home—those children will spend time with their fathers. Those children will learn from their fathers; they will be loved by their fathers. And for little boys, this is especially important—that they will be taught by their fathers.

As the boy grows into a teenager and starts to date, the father will tell his son about the importance of relationships, and soon guide him, tell him what to expect from marriage, how much that union can improve his life. There will be no question as to whether the son will want to get married, for the same reason that children of parents who have gone to college are more likely to go, or that the children of parents who are readers will probably develop a love for reading as well.

But what happens to the little boys when there is no father in the home? How do we grow up, and what will our opinions of marriage be?

Boys without a father in the home will wake up and sit at the table and eat breakfast with their mother, or alone with their siblings because their mother is off to work. Boys without a father present will have to rely on their mother to tell them about "the birds and the bees." But really, what mother wants to have that conversation with her son? And nowadays, do mothers even know at what age to have it?

When I was young, the average age a boy started thinking about, or actually having, sex was sixteen. Do you really think your son is waiting that long today? And if he hasn't lost his virginity by sixteen, considering the Internet, and raunchy music videos, and cable television porn, he probably knows more about sex than you do.

But getting back to the little boy growing up without a father, if there are "father and son" activities in school (which most schools don't even conduct anymore because so many fathers are absent), he won't participate in them.

There will be no father-and-son time around the house—the time when, as boys, we will look up to our father, try to emulate him, desire to be just like him when we grow into men. At this point in a boy's life, we will create our own definition of what *father* means, purely by the example we witness. But if there is no father there . . .

When we start to desire the attention of girls, we'll find a way to get that attention, and we'll find a place to give them our attention, whether in our mother's basement, in the backseat of our cars, or even behind the school.

Boys will use girls only to fulfill our sexual needs, and at that age, be it fifteen or sixteen years old, determine that girls have no other real importance.

After graduation from high school, when we go to college or start working a job, we will see women the same way. Why would we have a reason to change our minds? There was no father there to tell us, or teach us, about marriage. And no, I'm not saying that you, as the mother, could not inform your child, try to positively persuade him. But when the father is in the home, married to the mother, and speaks to his child about it, it's more than a suggestion. It becomes an endorsement, because the father is practicing what he preaches, living what he speaks. But if there is no father there, like there has not been for so many of the men who are of marrying age today, why would we want to marry? It certainly wouldn't be based on what we've seen. You might say that if we grow to love a woman, then we should want to marry her. But a man can love a woman for the rest of his life and still feel no need to marry her if he doesn't know the benefits, doesn't understand the reasoning behind it.

This is something that may cause us to move very slowly when considering taking steps in that direction, or leave us frozen.

So, does that mean that all is lost, that the generation of boys today will have just as much trepidation as the men of today because of the absence of their fathers? Yes, it could very well mean that. Or there could be something that you, as mothers, could do to eliminate that possibility.

Marketing marriage

If you're a single mother, how will your son find out about marriage?

If you're divorced, what's your son's opinion of marriage now? Did you know it while you were still married?

If you're happily married, your son is being raised by you and your husband. He sees the two of you every day, and if he's still a young boy, when he gets old enough to wonder, most likely there will be discussion as to how the two of you got married, and why.

But what if you have a son and you're not married? There will be no man to wonder about, to ask questions about, so there will be no discussion about marriage.

So how will he ever find out? Will you tell him about marriage?

You should. Believe it or not, by default, it is your responsibility.

Ask yourself, as a single mother, how often do you promote marriage to your son? Have you even discussed it, ever given him the definition of marriage? Ever felt the need to? Probably not.

Single women, be they those who have never been married or those who, for whatever reason, have gotten divorced, probably don't feel like breaking into song all of a sudden about the joys of marriage. If it was so great, you wouldn't have to promote it. You'd be married, and the promotion would take care of itself, the way it's supposed to. Right?

But for your son, it's a bad thing that you haven't had this discussion, that you haven't told him how wonderful a marriage union can be, even if yours flopped.

Why?

Think about how you were first introduced to marriage. If your parents are together, or at least *were* together, then you found out about it from them. But if you were raised by your mother alone, or even by just your dad, you probably were first introduced to the idea of marriage and weddings and two people falling in love by a cartoon, a children's book, or maybe a fairy tale, where the princess marries the prince at the end.

Later, your girlfriends talked about it, how they were going to marry their favorite teen idol. Girls look through wedding magazines and fantasize about the day they will one day be brides.

Boys don't think about stuff like that. Marriage, baby dolls, weddings—none of those things are promoted to boys. As kids, we're more interested in monsters than marriage, race cars than wedding rings.

I'm not faulting my mother, but I believe that if she were to have at least once sat me down and told me all the benefits there are to being married, how wonderful an institution it is, and that I should make it a goal in my life, just as she pushed me to get an education and follow my career dreams, I think I might be married now.

But ladies, know that it's never too late. If you're single and raising a son, or a daughter, for that matter, or if you've gotten divorced and your son is seventeen and about to leave the nest, or even if he's thirty years old and has been on his own for some time, schedule a mother-son talk with him. (Pick a day and sit him down and promote marriage as if it's the best thing since free cell phone long-distance calling.)

If you haven't done it already, do it. You owe him at least that, considering the damage you may have done him in the past without even knowing.

How you turn your son off to marriage

You're a single mom, so you're divorced, or for some reason you chose not to marry the father of your child. It could be because of something you did, or something he did, or it was just his decision not to take you as his wife, or at least stick around to raise his son.

He says his reasons were good ones. "I didn't know I'd have to be here all the time just to raise a kid," or, "If you told me you wanted to get married before I got you pregnant, I never would've had sex with you."

"Yeah, right!" you say.

But because of your child's father's departure, you have certain feelings about him, and maybe they are not pleasant feelings.

If that's the case, know that those feelings should always be kept to yourself. Never let your child in on them. If you look into your son's eyes and tell yourself he has eyes just like his good-for-nothing, lying, cheap, cheating scoundrel of a father, that might tempt you to say those things aloud. Don't do that.

If we know our father—and most times even if we don't (seeing a photo, or just knowing he's out there)—many of us boys still worship him. Although bashing him might make you feel good, it makes your son feel awful.

Your son will not only see the anger that's in you, but hear it, and feel it. Even though that anger is not directed at him, he'll tell himself he would never want to make you that angry at him. He'll also tell himself that he never wants anyone else to be that angry. To avoid that, he may tell himself he'll avoid what his father has done—having a child.

And if he tells himself he doesn't want children, and if he still believes that marriage comes first, that couples marry so that they can have children, he may tell himself that if he has no plan for kids, then there's no need for marriage.

Speaking badly about his father doesn't even make you feel good, does it?

All it does is make your son feel bad, and, believe it or not, makes you look bad.

And if you tell yourself you'll take that hit, knowing that at least you're informing your kids of what kind of rotten man they have as a father, abandon that theory, because it's not necessarily true.

My mother never said a negative word about my father, but his actions alone, before their divorce and after, always let me know he wasn't as good a man as he could've been and should've been.

But there's something else that you do that can make your sons less likely to want to marry.

Dating.

I know. You're a single mom, and you've been raising your son for the last two years, and you haven't had a date since. You're so wired that every time the sixty-five-year-old mailman drops off your letters, you wonder if he'd be down for ditching his bag and stepping inside for a quickie.

Your sole existence isn't just about being a mother, you tell yourself. You're a woman. You want a life, too!

The same goes if you've been married and now you're divorced. There's a point when you feel you want and need to get back out there and reacquaint yourself with the woman you once were. But you have that two-year-old at home, or that ten-year-old, or your twins who are twelve. Whatever the age, you've got kids, but not every guy should be introduced to them.

You understand all that stuff. But you still would love to have a conversation about something other than *Sesame Street*, and drink something harder than imaginary tea from your kid's plastic teacups.

So you meet a guy, go out on a date. You tell yourself you'll take it slow, and not invite the guy in and risk exposing your kid to him too soon. But eventually, he grows on you. You've been dating him for six months, and you tell yourself your son will like him.

You make the introductions. The guy starts spending nights at your place. Your son starts bumping into him in the middle of the night on the way to the bathroom. The guy is walking around your house in his underwear and tube socks like your son's father used to do, and, unbeknownst to you, your five-year-old son is like, "What the f*&% is going on?!"

One day, your new guy finally shows his true colors—does something unforgivable—and you end it, only to have to start all over again with someone else. Three months later, you're introducing your son to your new "friend," who'll eventually walk around the apartment in *his* underwear.

You have to know this is sending the wrong message to your son. And if you're trying in any way to promote marriage to him, this is the exact opposite of how it should be done.

When your son sees this guy, the guy you're dressing up for, cooking dinner for, giggling with and kissing on the cheek, the first thing he'll do is think about his father. He will tell himself that you put his dad out for this clown. But what's worse, rather than going through all the pain his father went through after the divorce, which all came from being married, your son will decide to just *date* women. As he would've witnessed by your example, he'll see that he'll receive all the benefits that a married man receives, but doesn't have to go through all the drama of a potential divorce.

So what do you do?

There's something you should always remember in regard to men. It's a blanket statement that pretty much covers all of us, and you can apply it to practically any situation. Make it your new golden rule.

If a man is interested, he'll let you know.

There it is. Now let me tell you how it applies to your dating issues.

Some men don't date women with children. If you're dating a guy now, he most likely isn't one of those guys, because you have kids and he's dating you, right? Then again, some of those guys make exceptions to their rule because of a specific interest they may take in you.

If you happen to have a guy who doesn't like kids, you'll eventually know it, because even though he's interested in you, he hasn't all of a sudden started loving children.

They know you have kids, but you'll find that they never ask about them. For Christmas, they will give you a gift, but will act as though your kid doesn't even exist. Your guy will never ask about your child, never want to spend time with him or her, and eventually you'll realize that, truly, his only interest is in you.

But you really like him, and you decide that you will introduce him to your kid anyway, and hope that something positive happens.

That's the worst mistake you can make.

Your guy will allow this to happen, because he knows he can't say, "I haven't asked about the little crumb snatcher, so I don't give a hog's balls about him." But that's what he wants to say. Remember the rule: "If a man is interested, he'll let you know."

You arrange the meeting. Your kid smiles, your man groans, then fakes a smile. Then, not long after that, everything goes right back to the way it was, only now your kid is tagging along in the backseat of his car everywhere the two of you go.

That man's opinion has not changed. He still doesn't like children, and isn't even trying to put up a front.

You're smiling ear-to-ear in the front seat, thinking how wonderful this is, when your child is in the back, knowing, sensing correctly, that this guy practically hates his six-year-old guts.

That doesn't mean that you can't ever introduce a man you're interested in to your kids. You just have to allow him to show an interest in a meeting first, and then you can decide if and when a meeting should happen.

If you've been dating a man for six months, or even three months, and he hasn't at least inquired about your kid, maybe asked when he could meet him, you should probably let that guy go.

If a guy you've been dating for only a month says he loves kids and he can't wait to meet your son, consider him a possible good catch. But most likely you should still make him wait, because you hardly know him yourself.

What I'm saying is, keep the number of guys you're interviewing for the "dad" position to a minimum. All it will do is confuse your son, and start to devalue the significance of relationships and marriage in his eyes. And you really don't want to do that, because marriage already gets so much of a bum rap from everyone else.

Bad word of mouth

Women gossip, but men impart knowledge. At least that's what we believe.

Men tell other men—our friends, our male family members, as well as our coworkers, or even the guy sitting next to us at the barbershop—things, give them information, in hopes that they will listen to what is told to them, learn from it, and maybe not make the same mistakes that we have made.

The sad thing is, some of the advice guys give other guys is stuff like, "You're so lucky to be single. I wish I never got married! And if you're considering it, think again."

Why would they say such a thing?

Maybe because they hate their marriage, and believe that by warning their friends, those guys might avoid what one guy believes to be the nightmare he can never wake up from.

You might say, okay, so one guy tells a friend or two never to get married. That shouldn't have that much of an effect on all the other guys who are considering doing it. No, it wouldn't if it was just one or two, or even two hundred, guys saying negative things about marriage. But it's so many more than that.

You're probably thinking, why would men listen to something like that?

Understand, sometimes it's not just our friends giving the warning. Many of our parents are divorced, men and women. If a guy still has a close relationship with his father after his divorce, depending on the experience the father had in the marriage (which, since he's divorced, we should assume was a negative one), he may tell his son that he might want to think twice about doing the same thing. Or even if his father doesn't say exactly those words, he may never again get married.

After divorcing my mother, my father never remarried, but continues to live with the same woman for decades. What kind of message do you think that sends to me and men like me?

Men listen, even if it is to the old guys at the barbershop, speaking to no one in particular about how evil and selfish their wives are. Single men have to deal with being told every day by married men how lucky they are to still be single, and that if the married guys could do it all over again, they'd never get married.

Now, don't get me wrong. All the guys I just mentioned who are still married probably love much that comes with marriage, possibly even most of it. But like I said before, men aren't quick to tell other men about things like that.

When was the last time you were on the bus or in the park and overheard a conversation between two men that went something like this:

"Aw, gee, I just adore my wife and love being married to her. Love and marriage are such wonderful things."

The other guy asks, "How long you two been hitched?"

"Ten great years," the first man says. "You really ought to do it. You don't know what you're missing."

"No, buddy, I do know. All my male friends say how fantastic they feel each morning they wake up, knowing they're married."

Most guys have never heard anything like that from another

man. I'm forty years old, and I've never heard anything remotely close.

But what we do hear from almost every guy who's been divorced is that he's never going to get married again. Or we hear how the woman he used to be married to took everything he had, married some guy ten years younger than him, and that they are living in the house the husband had built with his own hands.

Men are told by other men—by our friends, our brothers, our fathers—men we respect and trust—not to go marching down that aisle with you . . . or else.

Sure, some of us, probably most of us, don't allow a few cautionary tales spoken by obviously hurt men to stop us from going ahead with our decision to one day get married.

But if those words don't ultimately stop us, they definitely cause us to pause, stop, and think. They might even have us question that if all, or most, or even a few, of the men whom we trust most in this world tell us that marriage is worse than any torture man can ever imagine and to avoid it at all cost, maybe we should consider doing what they say.

CHAPTER TWO

Finding the Marriage-Minded Man

Before I start giving advice on what to do to get the attention of the man you might be interested in, let me introduce you to the five different types of guys you will run into. It's important for you to be able to identify them, and label these guys accordingly. In doing so, based upon what they expect from you, you will know if a guy is worth your time, and can make the informed decision as to whether to consider him for marriage.

The five types

The Ladies' Man (under 35):

This guy, as I stated in the opening of the book, is who I told you not to marry. You ask, why would you need me to warn you not to marry this guy if he's a Ladies' Man? That's common sense. But sometimes even these men will stumble upon such a great woman, they won't want to throw her back after they've landed her, afraid another man will hook her. This man knows he has no intention of being faithful in his marriage, but he wants to marry you because you're such a rare find. He's telling himself that he can still play around out there when he wants to as long as he takes care of you at home. And when he's finally ready to truly settle down, he would've already secured the good woman whom he knows he ultimately wants to be with. But don't fear, because this is not the Ladies' Man's main objective. His true goal is to stay "single," and date as many women as he can. Now, if you're dating with no immediate intentions of getting married, and you don't mind a man who you know will have a plethora of women, then there's nothing wrong with choosing the Ladies' Man. But if you know that you want marriage, even as late as five years from now, it's best that you stay away from this particular type.

I already know the next question you're going to ask. How will you know you're dealing with a Ladies' Man? Remember the new golden rule? If he's interested, he'll let you know. It still might take a moment for you to determine if you're dealing with a Ladies' Man or not, because he's so adept at disguising his motivations and his cheating. Unless you're careful, which you always should be, you might never find out. But like I said, if he wants a relationship with you, he'll pursue one. But, then again, most men will do that. How to really determine if you're in, or about to start, a relationship with a Ladies' Man is through longevity and consistency.

This guy is easy to reach when you first start dating, because he's trying to make an impression. He's trying to secure you, and he knows this is what you're looking for, and what you expect in a man. But wait until after you agree to have a committed relationship with him. If he's no longer available as much as he used to be, if his phone calls lessen, as well as his attentions, his mind and his efforts are going somewhere else. Walk away, and don't even feel guilty about not giving him an explanation as to why.

The Ladies' Man (over 35):

Okay, so this is a guy who is at the age where he should've stopped dating several women by now. He should be ready for just one woman, commit to her, and marry. This is the man who should've had his fill of sex-just-for-the-sake-of-sex relationships, but for a handful of reasons, he has not gotten to that point yet. One reason could be that running around, juggling women, playing the game, is still quite good to him. In his lifetime, this man has probably had a great deal of success in that arena, and feels that as long as he's still meeting his goals, there's no reason to stop. Eventually, men like these slow down, and come to the realization that they can't behave like this forever. But until then, give these men their room. Some of these men over thirty-five might not be interested in marriage because they've had failed marriages. If a man like this considers himself a Ladies' Man, it doesn't matter at what point after his divorce you meet him; his intentions are to avoid another marriage at all cost, and regardless of how good you are to him, no matter how well you love him, cook for him, clean for him, and support him, you will not be able to repair the damage done to him by his failed marriage.

How will you know if you have an older Ladies' Man on your hands? The same rule applies. If he's interested, he'll let you know. Many things change about men as we mature, but this does not. A sixty-year-old man will tell you what he wants from you just as quickly as a twenty-year-old. If he realizes he has no interest, he will distance himself from you before you even realize anything is wrong.

For men, with maturity comes a lack of patience. The older Ladies' Man is still in the game to get what he wants, and, unlike the younger Ladies' Man, he won't necessarily try to deceive you. Most, when asked about marriage, will often tell you point-blank that he's not interested. He's been married before, and it didn't work then, so he's not trying it again. He'll tell you that if marriage is what you want, he's not the man, so you should look elsewhere. Yes, it's kind of brash, bordering on rude, but he's doing you a favor. Take it, thank him, and move on.

The Marriage-Minded Man:

It doesn't matter how old this man is — he wants marriage, plain and simple, and nothing's going to stand in his way. This guy beautifully exemplifies the rule I've been talking about. You might have seen him in action. He's been bitten by the "marriage bug" and has come down with a serious case of marriage-minded sickness. Generally, guys afflicted with this disease will be older. You'll go out to dinner with him, and the moment the appetizer arrives, he'll go into a line of marriage-related questions: What do you think about marriage? Will you ever? Do you want kids? How many? Do you cook? Clean? Have sex more than three times a week?

Often, men like this aren't looking to marry a woman because he loves a particular woman and can't live without her, but simply because he's looking to get married. He's tired of eating Twinkies and soda for dinner. He's tired of stepping over the dirty clothes in his filthy bathroom, and thinks a wife will remedy that problem. He's getting married because it's time. But I shouldn't down him too much. Sure, he's also looking for love and a good relationship. He just wants it right now. If nothing else, he knows what he wants, and he has no problem letting you know it.

Fortunately for you, most Marriage-Minded Men aren't this far gone. These guys are tired of game playing, tired of mindless dating, and feel the same way you do. They're tired of wasting time. They want a relationship that will take them into the future. They want to know that the efforts they're making to befriend a woman, to love and treat her with respect, will last a lifetime. If you are seeking marriage, I don't have to inform you that this is the type of man you want.

How will you know if you've stumbled upon a Marriage-Minded Man? Easily. As I've been saying, he'll simply tell you. And it will be early on because, as I've said, just like you, he's not about wasting time. This man isn't trying to force you into a situation like the man with the marriage disease; he just wants to know if your expectations are the same as his, so he can decide if he'll continue to pursue you, or look for someone who is more serious about getting married.

The Middle-of-the-Roader:

Here's a guy who hasn't really made up his mind. He's the average guy, the guy who may have been raised by both parents in a loving home, and been presented with a good marriage model.

Or he could be just the opposite. He could have been raised by a single mom who downed his father every opportunity she had, and cursed even the idea of marriage from the time her child was breast-feeding to the day he ate his last meal under her roof. But for this guy, neither experience has determined what he will do in regard to marriage.

The Middle-of-the-Road guy tells himself he might marry; then again, he might not. Usually, everything has to do with the woman. If he finds a great girl, the time is right, and he falls in love with her—because he doesn't necessarily have anything against marriage—he'll marry her. And that's usually what happens. But because this man is indifferent, not pressured, not really looking for marriage, if he doesn't find that woman, there's a good chance he'll remain single. The Middle-of-the-Road guy is also a man you won't mind dealing with. You won't find this man proposing to you as quickly as the Marriage-Minded Man, but, then again, that's not necessarily a bad thing. Whereas the Marriage-Minded Man is getting married to a woman because marriage is what he wants, the Middle-of-the-Road guy is getting married because he wants *you*. There's a huge difference. But that's not to say the former will make less of a husband.

Now, how will you know if you're dealing with a Middle-of-the-Roader? There's nothing that will jump out at you. The quickest way to find out is just to ask him his thoughts on marriage. Most likely he'll say he hasn't decided yet. He'll tell you he could do it, but, then again, he may not. But that's a good thing. You know that he's at least open to the possibility. Unfortunately, you'll also know that if it's not you he chooses to marry, it wouldn't be because he doesn't like the idea of marriage; he just doesn't like you.

The Fearful Guy:

After the Ladies' Man, this is the guy you most want to avoid. Lucky for you, this is the man that this entire book is about, so if you happen to find yourself in a relationship with him, you'll have an entire book of instructions. The Fearful Guy is running, constantly looking over his shoulder, hoping some woman waving a wedding dress brochure isn't gaining on him.

I was in this category for more years than I want to admit, and I didn't care who you were, how beautiful you were, how great your body was, how much money you made—I wasn't marrying you. Because of my parents' failed union, because of all my friends who were in awful marriages, because of my friends who were getting hosed while getting divorced, and all the negative word of mouth I heard about marriage, I wasn't going to do it.

The Fearful Guy is spooked by everything I just mentioned, and more. He could have also been married in the past, divorced, and now is frightened to even think about going back there. The good thing is that this is usually a phase. As it was for me, men realize that if they want a fuller life, a family, a lifelong companion, they will have to get over their fear, man up, and start considering the possibility of marriage.

When does this happen? For a lot of us, I'll go back to that magic age of thirty-five, for so many men were Fearful Guys before then. If you're looking for marriage from a Fearful Guy, this is the only time you'll want to date him.

So how will you know if you're the unlucky woman who is dealing with a Fearful Guy before he's started to deal with his fears? This is a tricky one. With the other guys, you can just ask, and either get a straight answer or enough information to know if you're wasting your time. But with this guy, well, you should already know that no man is quick to admit that he's scared of anything. So he won't tell you he's fearful. But that doesn't mean he's against marriage, or that he hates the idea of it. Actually, for years, many Fearful Guys have thought about the possibility of it, telling themselves that if they found the right woman, the right circumstances, they would pull the trigger. The only issue is their fear.

So what do you do if you find yourself dating a Fearful Guy and you realize you love him and want marriage? Tell him. But know that your words may be falling on deaf ears. He may hear what you're saying, may nod his head and act as though he's taking it seriously, but if he's still fearful, in his mind he'll just be humming a tune, trying to drown out what you're saying. Knowing that, you have to not only let him know how you feel, but mean it. You also have to go one step further and give him a time limit, a deadline to shake whatever fear he may be dealing with.

You're probably thinking that this is going a bit overboard. It might be, but it's accomplishing at least two things. First, it's letting him know that you're serious. And second, it's telling him how much time he has to determine if he can get on the same page with you. If he's a decent man, he'll do a calculation in his head right there and tell you that, yes, he understands, and that he wants to continue seeing you, knowing exactly your position on the matter. On the other hand, he might tell you that he's not ready now, and that he knows he won't even be ready in the year or two that you were considering giving him. Either way, you win, because at least you know where you stand with the Fearful Guy, which is an accomplishment in its own right.

Now that you have a good idea of the different types of men you might find yourself dealing with, let's discuss dating, and what you should do when that guy you're interested in approaches. Then again, many of you wonder why the guy you might be interested in never approaches. Read on. I've got something for you, too.

The time is not right

I know what you ladies hate.

You're on the StairMaster sweating up a storm, got your earphones on, your iPod blasting, your long-sleeved shirt tied around your waist, draped over your backside, so guys can't take a look at your behind. Then some guy pops into your peripheral vision.

He pretends he's about to start an innocent workout, mind his own business, but you know he's not going to, because he chose the machine smack-dab next to yours when there were six others available.

Not two minutes pass, and he's tapping you on the shoulder, and you think—if I wanted to talk to you, man, do you think I'd be listening to my iPod?

Women hate that, and every one of us men who approaches you knows that.

The deal is, we step to you anyway. The reason? We might never see you again. I'm sure you've heard that before. It might sound like a line, but there's truth to it. We may not be a member of that gym. We might happen to be there that one time, and want to talk to you. Or there might be a guy who may not frequent that grocery store where he spotted you—and yes, your hair is in rollers, and men should know that's a red, flashing neon sign that screams, DON'T TALK TO ME! I'M NOT FEELING VERY ATTRACTIVE RIGHT NOW!—but if he approaches anyway, that means you are attractive to him.

I'm trying to make this point because so many women miss out on a number of potentially good men just because we approach you on the street, or on the bus, or wherever you think is not the right place, or the right time.

I had to explain this to a woman I tried to simply start a conversation with at the gym, on the stair climber, while she was listening to her iPod. She blasted me, scolded me like I was a child, so I had to defend myself. I told her that it's a man's responsibility to approach women.

Women make it hard; you make it frustrating. One minute you're tired of men coming up to you, bugging you. The next, you're griping because the cute guy you want to say something to you is just standing across the room, talking to his friends, taking sips from his martini, staring dead at you, but not making a move.

I know what it is. You're cool with the guys that you find attractive approaching, but you want the guys you find unattractive to stay away.

The problem with that is that men don't have access to what's in your head. We don't know if we repulse you or not. Even if you're beautiful, tall, thin, and swanlike, and we're fat, dumpy, and balding, we still think there may be a chance, because all the guys on television commercials and CBS sitcoms are dumpy and balding, but still have beautiful wives.

All joking aside, we have to find out for ourselves. And isn't that the way it's supposed to be? Imagine if men just decided that we weren't going to place our egos on the line anymore, that we were going to grant you women your wish, and not step up to you anymore—not on the bus, in the grocery store, anywhere. After a while, you would start looking at your butts in the mirror, asking your girlfriends if you've gained weight, and wondering why men don't find you attractive anymore.

Trust me, ladies, guys hate the cold call. We feel like telemarketers calling you right in the middle of dinner, or while you're in the tub, intruding on your most personal moments.

Knowing this, we still ask you to strike a deal with us. If we're able to make the attempt to speak to you, we believe you should at least honor us with a little conversation. Who knows, we just might be the man you're looking for.

When he does approach, know when to give
him time and when to blow him off

First, I'm going to do you ladies a huge favor, so no guy will ever call you the *B* word again. I think it's awful when a man resorts to that, but let me try to explain why they do. (For the record, I've never done it, and never will sink so low.)

Like I said earlier, we really put our egos on the line when we decide to walk up and speak to you. As you all should know, a man's ego is a very fragile thing. But for some men, it's not just his ego, it's his future.

Some women may have heard of this, and most of you may not have but among men, there is something known as the "eight-second rule." What this dictates is that upon seeing a woman we wish to speak to, we should approach her within eight seconds. The reason for this? you ask. If after seeing a woman, a man stands there, admiring just how beautiful she is, his mind will start to drift. He'll start to fantasize that this might indeed be the woman of his dreams. He'll start to see their future together all in a matter of moments. He'll visualize their relationship, the kids they could have, and just how happy a man he'll be because he no longer has to eat cereal for dinner.

When a man does that, he creates an insane amount of pressure, telling himself that all he has to do is be perfect, say exactly the right things, get her laughing, make her realize he's the man she's been looking for all her life, and then he'll be golden. But when she does start walking his way, he realizes there's no way he'll be able to pull that off, but he has to try anyway.

When he mumbles a very respectable "You look nice. How are you today?" and you look at him like he has three eyes, turn, and finish thumbing through your magazine—that's when he transforms into Mr. Hyde and drops the *F* bomb and the *B* word.

Is it right for us to resort to such harsh terms? Most of the time, no. But, then again, sometimes some of you women deserve to be cursed out. I hate to say it, but it's true. Some of you are so rude and think you're all that. You may have just come out of the beauty salon, just got your hair dyed, and curled, and you're wobbling around on your six-inch heels, with your skin-tight jeans, and no one can tell you anything. You *know* you're looking fine.

But it's still all about mutual respect.

Whether you feel like you're being bothered or not, when we present ourselves to you respectfully, when we go out of our way to say you look nice, that should still be perceived as a compliment.

And when someone pays you a compliment, what do you do?

You say, "Thank you."

Most women know this, but some of you don't. And some of us feel you must be reminded, and that's what we believe we're doing when we call you outside of your name.

Now, I'm not saying that you should speak to every man who says two words to you. Sometimes you are too busy, or you just don't feel like being bothered, or you aren't attracted to the man in the slightest. It happens. I understand.

So here's advice coming from a man on how to deal respectfully with men you don't wish to give the time of day to. This advice is for how to handle men who approach you as though they have some sense, not the guys who honk and yell out of open car windows as they drive by. This is not for the guys who approach you telling you how good they could make you feel in bed if you just gave them a shot.

I'm referring to the guy who sits down, places his tray in front of yours at the mall food court, and asks, "Do you mind if I eat lunch with you?"

It's not terribly original. It's not creative or clever or funny. It's not a riddle or a poem, or something one would find in a greeting card—all things that some women feel men should approach them with. It's just a simple request that deserves a simple answer.

If you like what you see, by all means, say, "Yes, have a seat."

If you aren't totally repulsed by him, if you're on the fence about whether you should or shouldn't, go ahead and let him sit down anyway. You might have the best lunch of your life.

But if you're pressed for time, or he smells like he hasn't washed in weeks, or you just feel like being alone, simply say, "I'm sorry, but I really just felt like being alone during my lunch break." Say thank you, letting him know that you appreciate his desire to spend time with you, then smile.

If you only knew how far this goes for us.

A smile from a woman—I mean, seriously. You could damn near curse us out, but if you show us a genuine smile while doing it, we'll walk away thinking, "But she smiled at me. There must be something she liked."

If a man approaches asking about your dating status, this is an easy out for you. Lie to him. Some men are very respectful about stepping to another man's woman. I'm one of those guys. If a woman wants to get rid of me, all she has to do is say, "I'm sorry, but I have a boyfriend."

I'll smile, ask her to forgive me for the intrusion, and tell her that her man is very lucky. No, I'm not crazy, or stupid. I know that she could be lying just to get rid of me, but, as most men should, I appreciate that she went to the trouble to let me down easy. Besides, I feel that if she does not want to speak to me, then I don't want to sit there and try to convince her. She's giving me an easy out, and I appreciate that.

Sure, there are many men who are pushy. They may come back with, "He doesn't have to know about me." Or, "We can just be friends. Give me your cell number and we can just talk on the phone."

If you aren't one to fall for that lame, elementary-type game, just say, "Would you like your girlfriend agreeing to just be friends with some man after she told him she was involved?"

There should be a moment of contemplation on his part, and then he should tell you that, no, he would not like that, and leave you alone.

If he continues pestering you, then it's fine for you to grab your tray, stand, and simply walk away. You've made your attempts to respectfully dismiss him. He would not go, so now you can take off the kid gloves. Ninety-nine percent of men will let you leave, knowing that they probably came on a little too strong. For the man who wants to be nasty and hurl a name at you as you go, simply keep on walking and let it hit you in the back.

I guess the important thing to keep in mind is that men will continue to walk up to you, asking for your phone number, when they find you attractive. All you have to know now is what to do when that happens.

When to give out your number, and when to take his

A man approaches you. He's smooth. You two have good conversation, he makes you laugh, and then he asks if he can contact you. How do you know when it's okay to give him your phone number? The answer is that you should never give it out upon the first meeting.

We ask you for your number because we truly want to contact you. If you give it to us, we'll definitely use it. But to tell you the truth, we'd rather not have to deal with the burden of calling you.

The game we used to play is, after receiving your digits, we wouldn't call you for two or three days. That'd make us appear as though we weren't pressed, as though we had other, more important things to do than think about calling you. This would give you time to simmer, fester, and worry if we really would call. When we finally did, you were supposed to be so happy to hear from us that we could basically have what we wanted, as long as we still showed some signs of interest.

Many women complained about this, and many men listened, deciding they'd rather do something different, because they weren't all about playing games anyway. Some men would call women the morning after getting her phone number.

"Hey, just wanted to say it was nice meeting you," he'd say to her, or leave a message on her voice mail.

Some men would call a day later, saying how interested they were in one day really getting to know the woman.

Men were trying to give you women what we thought you wanted, what you said you wanted. What we found out was that women thought that men who called not long after receiving your phone number were desperate. You believed we came off as too excited about the possibility of getting to know you, and that freaked you out a bit.

When you get a call from that guy, you'll listen to the voice mail, hear the enthusiasm in his voice, then pull the phone away from your ear, look at your girlfriend, and say, "Naw. I just gave this clown my number yesterday. He probably ain't had none in ages." And you never call the guy back.

I know, many of you are saying that's not true, but it is. I've experienced it firsthand.

Considering now that cell phone numbers are the ones mostly being exchanged, it's also a problem for the man to know exactly when to call.

A guy knows that the best time to have that first phone conversation is when the woman is settled in her own home, hopefully in the bathtub, relaxed, ideally working on her second glass of Merlot, and is without distraction.

But when calling a cell phone, we know you could be anywhere in the city; in the country, for that matter.

A man knows there's nothing worse than calling a woman for the first time, trying to have an intimate get-to-know-you conversation, while you're in the checkout line at Target, or on your way to a club with a car full of your girlfriends.

We know we get only one time to make that first phone impression. A great first phone call, lasting an hour or two, where there is talk about everything from politics to what each of you wants in the next five years to what turns both of you on in bed, could set both of you on the path to having a wonderful relationship.

Then again, we know that if we catch you at the wrong time, and after two short verbal exchanges you say, "You know what? Can I call you back when I get home?" that could end whatever chances we had at getting with you.

That's why when we ask you for your number, and you say, "You can't have mine, but I'll take yours," we pretend that we're disappointed, but truly, we prefer it that way.

Most of the time, we know as you walk away that you're going to toss our number in the trash along with the old gum you're tired of chewing. But a smart man is okay with that, telling himself that if you weren't interested in calling him, it's better that you didn't. And it's much better than him trying to call you, attempting to convince you to find him interesting when you couldn't care less.

Women also don't want to give their phone number out because they just might happen to hand it to the man who will not take no for an answer, that ax-murdering stalker you and your friends always joke so much about.

Many of you will give out your number, and when the man calls, you don't pick up the phone, because even while scribbling your name and number across that torn slip of paper, you never intended to. But he calls again and leaves a message, but you don't return it. So he calls, and calls, and calls, and a week and a half later, he's still calling like a bill collector on crack.

But the main reason why women should always take our number is because it gives you options, and it puts you in the position of power. If you take the guy's number just to get him off your back, then mission accomplished. You never have to call him.

If you thought he was the most attractive, funniest, best-built guy you ever met in your life, having his number frees you from worrying if he'll call you, or just toss your number in the top drawer of his dresser, like all the other phone numbers he retrieves.

Most important, you can make that phone call when you choose. That is, after you've had that second glass of Merlot and lowered yourself into that warm bubble bath.

And know this much, for us, we could be in the checkout line at Home Depot, in the strip club, or watching the last play of a double-overtime Super Bowl game, where the score is tied, time has ticked down to one second, and our favorite team is about to kick a fifteen-yard field goal. If we get that call from you that we've been waiting for, we will simply cover the mouthpiece and excuse ourselves in order to find a quiet place so we can talk. That is, if we're really interested. And if that conversation goes the way you want it, now give him your number and expect him to call you back.

So, my advice is that if numbers are being exchanged, for all the reasons I've stated, let the flow go from his hand to yours. But if you're considering taking his number as just a quick way to dismiss him, I'd say go ahead and tell him that you aren't interested. In this case, being honest is better than leading him on, having him running to his cell phone every time it rings, thinking it's you. You've been in that position before, and you didn't like it. Why would you want to do that to someone else?

So now that you know what to do when that cute guy asks for your number, what do you do if he doesn't?

That cute guy is checking me out, but he won't say anything

How many of you women have been in this situation? Probably all of you at one time or another, and most of you did nothing about it but complain afterward to your girlfriends on your way home from the bar.

Some of you may have been bold enough to actually walk over there, say something crazy, like, "I saw you checking me out, and I just wanted to come over and say hi," only to realize that the man had a lazy eye, and he was no more interested in you than in your fat girlfriend. You turn, shamefully lower your head, and retreat to lick your wounds.

I know most of you aren't going to put yourself in that position for just that reason, even if you see the man of your dreams, even if you know he would be perfect. You'd rather stand there pressed up against the wall of that club, sipping from your Sex on the Beach, or push that shopping cart through the deli section for the fifth time, hoping he finally says something to you, before you "woman up" and say something first.

I find this hilarious, and want to say, welcome to our world.

Now you know how it feels to be in the position of risking paying for what you want with your ego. To have to lay on the line every ounce of your self-confidence, and possibly have some man look at you, laugh in your face, and tell you to run home before your owner misses you and starts tying flyers to the streetlamps because he lost his dog.

This is all in your head. I mean, really, how many women actually get shot down like this? And to tell you the truth, if it has happened like that, that particular girl probably had no business walking up to that particular man in the first place.

If you are even halfway decent—and when I say halfway, I mean you have both arms and legs, don't have a beard, or at least shaved within the last two days, and don't weigh fifty pounds more than the man you're trying to talk to—we won't shoot you down. Hell, most guys might still give you their number, because it so rarely happens to them.

I was talking to my sister about this. She asked me what she should say to a man she finds attractive.

My answer: "Boo." "Cat." "Dog." "Bow-wow."

My sister is attractive, so no man would look at her, turn his nose up, and keep on walking after she made even the lamest attempt to get his attention.

But the woman who steps to a man doesn't have to be that attractive, because, as I said before, since women don't walk up to us every day, starting conversation, we're so blown away, so appreciative, we're going talk to you.

Then, if we sense you're attracted to us, we're going to start looking you over. What's happening now is the categorization process. If you're very attractive, we're telling ourselves, okay, this could be my future wife, or my girlfriend, or someone I could replace my present girlfriend with. If you're not so attractive, we start checking out your body, and might tell ourselves, no, I won't always be able to stare her in the face, but she has a nice rack, or a nice behind—she could be my Tuesday night girl, or maybe even Thursday.

Bottom line, we aren't going to squander a situation where all the work is done, where we know the woman is interested, just because she doesn't have a shelf of beauty pageant trophies in her bedroom. She's eagerly applying for a position, and even if she is underqualified, most men will definitely find somewhere to place her where she'll work out just fine.

Ladies, I guess what I'm trying to tell you is not to ever fear walking up to a man and saying whatever you want to him.

I was speaking to a guy about this, and of course he agreed that women should never hesitate approaching us, but he made a good point in that we have to be careful about how we approach you. A man doesn't want to run up behind a woman, or rudely lean over her shoulder while she's out having dinner with her girlfriends. If we were to run behind you and squeeze into the revolving door without your permission, the average woman would probably scream bloody murder, and maybe have a right to.

Men, on the other hand, because we're just naturally bigger, don't worry too much about that. If we're dining alone, you can pull the empty seat out at our table, sit down, stare us in the face, and say, "What's up?" And we'd most likely just smile and ask if you'd like to join us.

So, to answer my sister's question more seriously—if a man is standing outside, waiting for a ride, or walking his dog, a woman can simply say, "Nice day, huh?"

If he's in a bar having a drink, you could say, "What's that? It looks good."

In the grocery store, look in his cart and tell him, "All that healthy stuff. I need to shop more like you."

Or, if you're just so dumbstruck by how handsome this man is, ask him for his help. It could be regarding anything—directions, lifting something heavy to put in your basket, or advice. While at a club, walk over and say, "My girlfriend and I were having a debate about___, and I wanted to know what you think."

Men always want to feel needed, and we believe that if we offer a hand, there's a chance we might get something back in return.

When he answers your question, even if it's the worst answer anyone could have possibly given, thank him. Same goes for when he's finished the task. Thank him, and then say, "Well, now how do I repay you?"

It's a wrap after that. If the man is the slightest bit interested in you, he'll suggest something that requires the two of you and some sort of alcoholic beverage. Bottom line, approaching a guy, striking up a conversation, and letting him know you're interested in him is probably the easiest thing you'll ever do; that is, if you frequent places where there are guys who are worth approaching. If you don't know where that is, let me make a suggestion:

Get a gym membership and lose the earphones

One way to bump into that guy while doing yourself a huge favor is to get a gym membership. If you don't have access to facilities at your place of employment or your school, then this is a must-have for every woman and every man.

Of course, the main reason is obvious: to stay fit. No one wants someone who is sloppy and out of shape. So get the membership because exercising reduces stress and makes you feel better in general. But as you begin to work yourself into better shape, your confidence will increase, and you'll also feel more self-assured in those situations we talked about when a man approaches, or when you approach him. Not to mention that your health will improve, allowing you to live a longer, more satisfying life.

But there is also the social benefit of joining a gym.

There are many complaints from women who work out in coed gyms. "Men are always coming on to me when all I'm trying to do is get a workout." Or, "The gym is nothing but a meat market. I wish those guys would just leave me alone."

Those gripes are coming from women who are already in relationships or are married.

But what about you? If you happen to be single and looking, these are exactly the types of complaints you want.

You ask, why would you go to the gym to catch a man? Isn't that lame? And going to the club isn't? At the club, you pay a cover just to get in. Yes, you pay a membership at the gym, but remember, your true reason for being there is for your health, and almost no price is too high to pay for good health.

When going to a club, you have to get dressed up and do your hair, when all you have to wear to the gym are sweats and a hair scarf.

While at the club, you buy countless drinks, stand by the wall with your girls, trying to look sexy, and hope some good-looking guy approaches.

At the gym, you handle your business by working out, and if some guy approaches, you'll fit in conversation between reps, or talk to him without stopping your twenty minutes on the StairMaster or treadmill.

If no one does approach, you leave after having a great workout, building your confidence and burning some calories. If a man doesn't approach you and your girls at the club, you leave after spending money for admission, money for drinks, and wasting a Friday or Saturday night, and part of the next morning, trying to recover from that head-banging hangover.

So now that I convinced you of the benefits of visiting the gym as opposed to going out to a club, let me give you some tips on what to do once you get there.

Prepare yourself. If you're attractive, men are going to approach you. Why would you think otherwise? We like beautiful women in good shape, so if you fall into that category, don't act surprised or pissed off when we stare or walk up to you.

Another thing: if you don't mind the idea of a guy trying to hold a conversation with you while you're working out, please, please,

please, lose the iPod and earphones as well as the butt wrap. And you ladies know what I'm talking about.

Some of you walk into the gym like you're wearing a suit of armor. Like your magic sweater wrapped around your hips will make your butt invisible, and those earphones stuffed into your head will repel men from saying a single word to you.

The sad thing is that the earphones do actually repel most of us.

There's nothing worse for a guy than having to physically tap you on your shoulder, grab your arm, or use some form of sign language, asking you to get rid of the earphones so we can speak to you. It's awkward, it throws off our game, and some of you know it. As I said, generally, these are women who are already involved.

But for those who aren't in a relationship, know that going without earphones allows for spontaneous conversation. You could be walking to the water fountain, and a guy might see you and say, "You must drink a lot of that, because you have great skin." If your headphones were pushed into your ears, you wouldn't have heard that, because the guy most likely wouldn't have said it.

So go to the gym and have the right attitude about it. It's not a meat market just because we approach you there. If that were the case, your place of work would be a meat market, as well as the grocery store, and anywhere else we see an attractive woman.

The last, but by far not the least, important reason you need to go: men love women who are in shape and take care of themselves.

Don't get the wrong idea. You don't have to have 6 percent body fat to be in shape. In shape doesn't mean you can't carry a few pounds around. Some of us even prefer women with some extra meat on their bones. But we have to know that you won't continue to pack on even more meat.

When men see a woman who works out, we know that at the very least she has the power, and the desire, to maintain the level of health she's at, if not even the desire to improve it.

If you aren't in perfect shape, it's no big deal, because we know that you're at least trying, as opposed to the woman who is overweight or out of shape, and instead of seeing her at the gym five days a week, we spot her at McDonald's or Wendy's.

So get that membership, leave the iPod in your bag, and wait for some guy to start asking you out. But when he does, I have another valuable piece of advice for you:

Never do dinner on the first date

So that guy approached you by the free weights. He had a nice smile, a good game, and got you laughing, so you asked for his number, and you called him. The two of you spoke on the phone a handful of times, he invited you out to dinner, and you accepted.

Let me tell you what he's thinking. If he really likes you, he's trying to think of the nicest restaurant within his budget he can take you to. He's going to try his best to make a good first impression, because he knows that opportunity comes only once. So he picks you up at your house and engages you in awkward, get-to-know-you conversation until you arrive at the restaurant.

The place is beautiful, you think, as you're escorted to your seats. And as you sit, you tell yourself he must be planning on spending a pretty penny. You relax, and he obviously does the same, because the conversation gets better. He even flirts some, and you're starting to feel the way you felt when you met him at the gym.

But after you order, after your date tells the waiter to bring a bottle of wine, you all of a sudden get a good whiff of his breath, and it's so bad, you feel you're about to pass out in the basket of bread.

What to do? What to do?

You don't feel like taking a cab home, and you are starving. So you decide to stick it out and hope for the best. After a painful dinner and several bad-breath-induced dizzy spells, he drives you home, parks in front of your house, turns off the engine, and stares at you, licking his lips.

"Thanks a lot. I really enjoyed dinner," you lie, your hand already on the car door handle.

He smiles, but he's giving you a look like he wants something more. At best, he expects an invitation inside your place, and at worst, a sloppy open-mouth kiss, neither of which you're feeling.

But before you go asking yourself, who does he think he is, let me tell you who this guy is.

He's the guy who just spent $75 or $125 on dinner. He's the guy who asked you out, and you're the woman who enthusiastically said yes. He's the guy who has been staring all night at the cleavage that you intentionally planned to display to him by wearing that off-the-shoulders dress. And now that he's all wound up, he wants you to help him straighten that coil just a little bit.

The deal is, as men, we put a lot of weight on those dinners. We try our best to impress you with them. But lately, we've been feeling that those dinners shouldn't just be given out for free, because nothing is really free anymore. So afterward, while parked in front of your house, that guy you never want to see again might lock the doors, close his eyes, and pucker up, expecting to get paid for the $125 he just shelled out.

Bad breath or not, after all of that, most men believe you owe us more than just a firm handshake.

But let me tell you, there is such an easy way to avoid all that mess: the coffee shop date. That's right, a coffee shop, and preferably one in a bookstore. This takes care of so many issues facing both the woman and the man.

A coffee shop is a much more relaxed environment. The pressure to impress is not nearly as high as it would be in an expensive, dimly lit restaurant. The time commitment is cut in half, and by much more if you choose.

First, you're not going to have a guy pick you up from your house to take you to the bookstore for coffee. You're going to drive your own car, which is a good thing, because you can leave whenever you feel good and ready.

You really couldn't pull that off if you allowed a man to pick you up and drive you to dinner. You would have to wait until he was ready to take you back home, or take a cab, neither of which you'd want to do if you were having a horrible time and wanted to leave quickly.

If you'll permit me the bad analogy, getting taken out to dinner at a nice restaurant is like buying a year-long cell phone contract, where despite how bad the service may be, or how many dropped calls you experience, you're stuck with that service.

The coffee shop is like a Boost Mobile, or pay-as-you-go contract. If the guy doesn't do anything for you, or if he's a jerk, or you just aren't feeling the flow, you can cancel that moment and walk out.

Believe me, men will appreciate this option much more as well. His check will total nothing more than the cost of two specialty coffees, and maybe a cookie. Even after a coffee shop date, he may still ask you for a kiss afterward (though I doubt that). But if he does, and you reject him, he won't feel as though he was robbed.

And if you really want to put the guy to the test, arrive a little early. Walk through the bookstore, grab a few books on things that interest you, or even topics that you want to know if he's familiar with, like politics, the environment, or business. Have them at the table you're sitting at, and strike up a conversation about those topics. He might just be another good-looking guy, or he might actually have something serious to say, and you might find yourself having the time of your life.

If that happens, the next date can be dinner at a nice restaurant, and you can do something I suggest all women try at least once.

Pick up the check; it's worth it

"Why would I do that?" you may ask. "He asked *me* out!"

But you answered the question and you didn't even know it.

That's exactly why you pay, because he asked you out, and he wasn't expecting you to pick up the check.

What I will say is this: do it only if you have a great time. If the guy you just had dinner with gave you one of the best first-date experiences you've ever had, making you sure you want to see him again, pick up the check. If you really feel that way, it would almost be crazy not to go ahead and dig inside your purse, pull out your credit card, and cover the expense.

Let me tell you why.

It will say to that man that you're interested, that you're the real deal, and that you want to be taken that way. Sure, you can give him a kiss, let him squeeze you in places normally reserved for the second, or even third, date. That should send the same message, and you can pocket that fifty or sixty bucks to go toward those new shoes you wanted. But why do that when every other woman is thinking the same thing?

If good men are as rare as most women say they are, why not do what will have you stand out?

Considering all that, imagine if you picked up the check on the very first date. Of course, you know the guy will be a gentleman and tell you not to even think about it. He's got it. But if you truly want to make that good impression, you will insist on paying. And don't say, "Okay, then let's go Dutch."

Although it hurts our wallets a little less, men are turned off to a woman who suggests going Dutch. We think you're taking care of all your expenses so that at the end of the date, if we happen to ask for a kiss, or ask to come in, you'll turn and look at us and say, "Why? I don't owe you a kiss or an invite in. I paid my own way, remember? Oh, yeah, and here's the receipt to prove it!"

So go ahead and pay for the entire meal, and even leave the tip. That is, only if you had a great time, you're interested in seeing this guy again, and you want to make an impression that will have him thinking about you long after the date is over. And it will also jet you to the front of the line of all the other women he's dating.

I really wonder why women don't do this more often, to tell you the truth. If this guy is so great—if he runs his own company, opened every door for you, pulled out your chair to seat you, then stood when you left for the ladies' room, and stood when you came back—why wouldn't every other woman out there want a piece of him, too?

So, if you were to actually drop a little cash and buy that first meal because you had such a wonderful time, we'd believe you were making a statement that says, "I had a great time. I think you're a terrific guy, and by paying for this meal, I'm showing you this token of my appreciation. I'm letting you know that I'm investing in seeing just where this can go, and I hope you feel the same."

So, he was blown away by your act of selflessness, so much so that he asked you out four more times to dinner—for all of which he picked up the check. The dates were great, but what you want to know next is, what do you do to take things to the next level?

Bake what your mama taught ya—cook for that man

Okay. Already, I know many of you are frowning at the notion I want you to cook for some guy you just met. Let me say in advance,

I'm going to advise this a few more times. To a lot of you, these suggestions and the remarks I make about a woman cooking may sound old-fashioned or even chauvinistic. Let me apologize for now, for that is not how they are intended. Cooking for your man means more to him than I'm sure many of you will ever know. Only for that reason I continue to mention it. Your willingness and desire, or lack thereof, could make the difference in your relationship ending or being taken to the next level. With that said, let's continue.

It surprises me how many women today are against cooking for a man they recently started dating. To tell the truth, more women than I thought rarely cook for the man they've been in lengthy relationships with.

I know some of you believe that cooking a man a meal on a fifth or sixth date is giving him too much, making yourself appear far too willing to please. And yes, I will agree. You don't want to grant just any man this kind of honor too early in the process. You don't want the guy you're interested in to think that you do this for every man you start dating, and you want to make sure the guy is even worthy of you standing over a hot stove.

But if he's passed the probation period with flying colors, however long that is, then there should be no hesitation in stirring a few things up in a skillet.

What I want you to ask yourself is, what damage does it really do?

The norm is for a man to take you out on three or four dates before you even think about asking him to your house. We're not being cheap, but the way we see it, by that time, we're out of easily a couple of hundred bucks, and we still don't know what's going to become of us. But we continue to throw money at you so you think we're generous, crack jokes so you'll believe we're humorous, and act as polite as possible so you'll consider us gracious.

Meanwhile, you can at least give that new guy you're dating a sign, let him know that he's doing all the right things by inviting him by so you can prepare a meal for him.

I guarantee you that his eyes will light up, he will be so surprised that you offered such a thing.

There are many women who will give bad advice, saying never cook for a man before you've been dating three to six months. If you cook for him too soon, he'll get used to it.

No, he won't.

If you cook for him every single time he eats, he'll get used to it. But if you cook for him on the fifth or sixth date, he'll just be introduced to the fact that you can cook, and that you like him enough to do it for him.

He's not going to "get used to it." He's not going to expect it every time he sees you. But if you're good, that man will definitely enjoy it on the occasions you do decide to cook.

So if that's the case, ladies, if you know, or at least heard, that the way to a man's heart is through his stomach, why don't you fry some chicken, or bake a cake? You may not know this, but a cooking woman says things to a man, appeals to him in ways a noncooking woman, or a reluctant cooking woman, doesn't. Well, what if I can't cook? you ask. Buy a cookbook. If you can read, you can cook. Making the effort is much better than saying you just won't cook for him. And don't worry if you burn the water on your first try. The more you cook, the better you'll get.

Cooking is important, because a man whose mother cooked for him all the time is accustomed to a warm, well-made meal, and he's hoping to find a woman who will do the same for him.

So I really want to stress how important this is, how huge the impression you'll make on your man if you do cook for him.

Again, I say, this may sound chauvinistic, but in the same way you may think it extremely manly for a guy to fix your car, clean your gutters, or haul furniture into your basement, in almost no other way does a man see a woman being more womanly than when he witnesses her in the kitchen cooking for him. Maybe it is because our mothers have done this for us for so long. We know she loved us more than any other woman, so we see the act as an example of love.

It might be that. It might be more than that. But if you're willing, and you're good, that man will put a check on his marriage list, and will hope that you score high in all the other areas.

If you aren't willing to cook, or look at him as if he just made a pass at your brother when he asks you to prepare a meal for him, that man will put down your refusal as a negative when it comes time to consider you as the one he wants to marry. A man who is ready to settle down looks into the future. We think about the holidays, and imagine the woman who doesn't want to cook in the kitchen microwaving macaroni and cheese, or dropping paper bags of Boston Market turkeys on the dining room table, and calling it Christmas dinner.

We don't want that.

We want a woman who's going to start cooking at three A.M. the morning before the holiday, like our mothers did, like our grandmothers used to.

We want a woman who knows how, and is willing to, prepare delicious and nutritious food for our kids, so they won't have to microwave individually wrapped hot dogs for dinner.

And in keeping with staying ahead of the next woman, cooking definitely separates you from many of the women who might possibly be vying for the same man's attention. I think that's why so many women suggest that other women don't cook for their men. Those women may not know how to, and want the playing field evened. By not giving that man what you know he wants, by not displaying a talent and skill that men place high up on the "what she's got to have" list, you're giving all those other women more of a chance.

I know you're probably saying, "But I'm giving him sex. What more should he want?"

Ladies, understand this: every woman who we deal with will give us sex. She knows that is not a negotiable point. But will every woman cook? No. So in knowing that, many of us are more appreciative of a woman who will cook us dinner on that fifth or sixth date than the woman who will simply spread her legs.

And last, if you don't want to cook for him, you're letting him know that you aren't very interested.

You say that's not true, but consider this. Tell a man there's something that you would like him to do. I'm not talking about flying to Africa and digging up a 6-carat diamond ring to present to you on your third date. I'm talking about something you know he's capable of. Let's say there's a door you want him to hang, or a lock you want him to change. You really do need it done, but this will also tell you if he has handyman skills, which I know women think is a definite plus.

"Would you mind changing the lock on my front door?" you ask him.

"No, no, no," he replies, wagging a finger in your face. "I could," he adds. "I know how. But it's only our fourth date. I change that lock, then every time I come over here, you're going to ask me to hang ceiling fans, fix your refrigerator, and tile the kitchen floor. You're going to get used to it."

A man won't say that. We see doing what you ask of us as an opportunity to prove our usefulness to you. But we also do it because we know how much you'll appreciate it.

Wouldn't you want to do the same for him, by cooking him a meal?

Again, ladies, give yourself an edge, because sex can take you only so far. It just isn't enough to keep a man. And sometimes the truth is:

Men lose interest in women only after having sex on the first date, because he was never interested in *you* to begin with

Let's say you met a great guy while you were out shopping. He was kind, caring, and funny. He suggested you come to his place.

You told him that would be great. Stepping into his house, you realized he was neat, had a great sense of style, and had money. It was undeniable by the quality of his furniture and the size of the flat-screen TV. He served you wine. The two of you listened to music, talked, and laughed, and during that time you kept staring at his lips, because you wondered what it would feel like to kiss him.

He wasn't crazy or blind, and said, "You want to kiss me, don't you?"

The two full glasses of wine you had gave you the courage to nod your head and say, "Yes, I do."

And the games began.

He was unclasping your bra, you were unzipping his jeans, while the two of you were rolling around on the sofa. Meanwhile, as your body was getting hotter, your brain was asking you if this was what you really wanted to do. It quickly answered back—of course, that's why your hands were ripping off his shirt.

Many of you find yourself in this situation, on the verge of giving up the goodies on the first date, and many of you ask that age-old, ridiculous question, If I do have sex with him, will he respect me in the morning?

Woman, please! Respect you? He doesn't even know you. And why are you even thinking about the morning? The fact that the two of you don't really know each other will become painfully obvious once the sex is over. He'll be lying next to you naked, with nothing to say, because all of that lively, witty, funny conversation was just in the effort to get to the panties, and since that was accomplished, he really has nothing more to talk about.

So after you make an attempt at a lame conversation starter, like, "I really love the color you painted your ceiling," he'll turn to you and say, with an exaggerated yawn and stretch of his arms, "Well, I'm really getting tired. I have to get up early for work tomorrow."

You know that's the hint to grab your crap and go.

But while you're plucking your panties off his bedroom carpet, you ask yourself, did you just blow it? You had a shot at a potential great relationship with a wonderful guy, and did you just throw all that away by spreading your legs too quickly?

The answer is absolutely not. You never had a shot at a relationship with him to begin with. The reason why I say that is because your first date with him was at his house.

Ladies, understand this. The moment a guy asks you to come to his house, or asks to come to yours for the first date, you know exactly where he wants his dealings with you to lead.

And where is that? you ask. The bedroom, of course.

Like I said before, when a woman steps up to us, or when we approach one of you, we know exactly what we want to do, and how we want you to fit into our lives. If we see a woman with a gorgeous body, but she might require a veil if we take her out in public, we know we're just approaching her to try to have sex. So if a man asks for a home visit on the first date, I hate to tell you this but he's putting you in the "veil" category.

Listen, if a man wants to start a relationship with you, he's going to want to impress you. He's going to want you to think him a perfect gentleman. He's going to want to create wonderful memories with you from the start. So that man will suggest a very nice restaurant on that first date. Or a walk along the lake or through the park at sunset. He wants an opportunity to speak with you, get you laughing, hoping that you will . . . well . . . fall in love with him.

Is that to say that he won't eventually want to rip your panties off with his teeth? Of course he will! But he wants you for so much more than that. So on that first date, he will try to do everything he feels a woman wants her man to do.

Am I saying that if you do have sex with a man on the first date, he won't ever consider having a serious relationship with you?

No, I'm not saying that. I had a relationship with a woman for five years after a first-date sexual encounter. But that is the exception, definitely not the norm.

I'm just giving you this information because I think it'll make things so much easier for you when you're on that first date, and that new guy is pushing down your jeans, and your mind is going crazy, conflicted with the decision about whether you should have sex or not. If you're wondering if he will respect you afterward, you'll now have the answers.

And here they are:

There is no question of respect. He's never had it for you, or he wouldn't have made the sexual pass at you after knowing you for only one day. And as to whether you should have sex: If you like the guy and you're cool with being a sex toy, I say, why not? That's the only way you'll see him again, because that's all he wants you for anyway.

CHAPTER THREE

Women and Children

How men feel about another man's child

If a man approaches you today with an interest in trying to date you, it seems more and more common that one of the first questions he might ask you is if you have any children.

For the man who doesn't have any of his own, he is probably holding his breath while he waits for your answer. He might be smiling, trying to make you believe he thinks the thought of you having a child or two is sweet, but he's really biting the inside of his lip.

If you say that you don't, the smile will become more genuine, and he'll exhale and tell himself he can continue to try to get to know you. If you tell him you do have children, he'll force that phony smile even wider and put on his routine, asking you how old they are, and what sex they are.

Most times, and I know this sounds harsh, but if he doesn't have children of his own, and he's truly looking for a serious relationship that might lead to marriage, he couldn't care less what you have. He's probably figuring out what he can say to end the conversation so he can stop wasting his time.

Like I said, this sounds quite harsh, but if you think about it, he's really doing you a favor. If there was something that you knew was a deal breaker when it came to dating a man, would you just overlook it and hope for the best? Of course not.

Men who consider women with children a no-no sometimes have good reasons for feeling this way. Among other things that I'll address a little later, some men feel a woman's child can place limitations on a new relationship. Women with children cannot be as spontaneous as a woman who can pick up and go whenever she wants. Arrangements must be made with either a babysitter or her mother or the child's father, which can be a drag at the beginning of a relationship, when all the guy wants to do is see the woman as often as he can.

But it's not like you're going to pack up your kid and send him to Arizona to live with his grandparents just because a guy would prefer that you have more time for him. I'm not suggesting that.

Ladies, I know you're proud of your children, and you might think that everyone in the world should love them as much as you do. Maybe, for you online daters, that's why some of you choose to post pictures with your child in your profile.

I know the message you're trying to send—no, the message you're very successfully sending—"To all men—I have children, and if you have any desire of getting with me, know that this is a package deal. If you aren't ready to be a father, then you can't be my boyfriend. If you expect to get in my panties, then expect to change some diapers."

But all men aren't without children. I'd even venture to say that most men over the age of thirty-five have at least one child. And that, of course, makes things easier for the woman who has kids of her own.

Men who already have children are much more accepting of women in the same situation. They understand what it is to raise a child, to love that child, to sacrifice for that child.

Some women with children have told me they will consider dating only men without children. Personally, I think that's pretty ridiculous. And as a mother, if you wanted to choose the easier route, I would say men who have kids is the way to go.

When you first meet and he asks you if you have kids, as opposed to holding his breath while waiting for your response, when you tell him yes, the man with children won't all of a sudden lose interest. Often, he'll gain interest, and before the conversation is over you'll find that the two of you are swapping stories about how crazy your kids can be.

But that doesn't mean that just because he has kids there's a guarantee he'll get along with yours. That also doesn't mean that just because a man doesn't have any children of his own he *won't* get along with yours.

It just happened that way with me.

Years ago, I went out on a date with a very attractive woman I had been trying to start something with for quite a long time. When I first met her, and first tried to date her, she had no children. Years later, when I found her again, she was raising a son she had with some guy she was no longer dealing with.

Anyway, the kid was three or four years old, and I was still interested in the woman, despite the fact that she had a child—and it was a little boy, to boot. (More on importance of girl versus boy later.)

I asked her out, and eventually she accepted, under the condition that we take her son with us. Okay, not a problem. How difficult can a four-year-old be? I thought.

I picked her and her kid up, and the little boy was wisecracking me all the way to the pizza place. Needless to say, as I was gripping the steering wheel, trying to contain my irritation with this boy, the mother was laughing as if the kid were the next Chris Rock.

We sat down at the restaurant, and I saw that I really wasn't having a conversation with the mother; that dinner really wasn't about us, but about how I interacted with the child. I was having the conversation with him, and the mother was acting as some sort of interpreter, defining some of the words he was butchering, or the words I couldn't understand, because he had a crayon in his mouth.

I felt like a fool, because I knew this was nothing but an audition. And I sat there and played along, trying to come off as funny, as though I cared about the little snot, when I really just wanted to knock him right out of that booth.

I ordered a medium pizza because I knew the mother was conscious of eating so late. I wasn't terribly hungry, so I figured it would be large enough.

The little boy started yanking pieces from the pan, biting through them like a piranha, and tossing the crusts onto his plate. I forfeited one of my pieces so the kid could have a little more to eat, but after he finished, he still looked as though he could've had another six or seven slices.

Later, the question came up as to what the boy should call me. I told the mother "Mr. Marcus." The woman almost went insane because I felt there should be some formality in how the child should address his elder.

"He shouldn't have to call you *Mister!*" she said. "Why does he have to do that? Why can't he just call you by your first name? He calls all my other male friends by their first names."

"He should call me 'Mister' because he's four, and considering that not long ago he just stopped crapping in his pants, he needs to do what people tell him to do," I informed her.

That didn't go very well.

I took the two of them home, and a week later, when I called the woman again, she was laughing on the phone, telling me how her poor boy was starving when they got home, and that she had to feed him all over again. She didn't come right out and say it, but I felt that she was implying that I was cheap because I didn't purchase the mega-giganto pizza, so the boy could fill his stomach, and then have some to take to school for lunch for the rest of the week.

As I did then, men often wonder, is it our responsibility to pick up the tab for your child when it's you we're trying to date?

The financial burden of your child

Here's an awkward situation. You go out on a date with a man and you bring your kid along. The two of you decided you wanted to see a movie. But when he goes to purchase the tickets, he asks only for two adults. After paying, he turns and gives you your ticket, obviously expecting you to pay the entrance fee for your own child. What would you do?

Yeah, I know. Most of you would rip your ticket in half, throw it in the guy's face, grab your kid's hand, and demand he take you home, if you don't start walking away because you're so pissed off.

But maybe you should ask yourself first, why are you pissed off?

If the man asked to take you out and you decided to invite your child because you thought it would be a great opportunity for him to get to know this guy, then there was no guarantee that he was going to pay for your kid.

But the real question is—should men pay?

Many of us feel we shouldn't, or at least that we should not have to.

Women shouldn't assume that just because we are trying to date you, we're willing to dig a little deeper in our pockets to date your child, too. Many of us feel that your child is your responsibility. We were nowhere to be found when the child was conceived, yet we are supposed to buy him a kid's meal when we buy you a burger and a shake?

On the other hand, many of us are cool with picking up the tab for the children of the women we date, at least for a while. Some of us choose to date women with children, and we know it's what's expected of us. At the very least, for the first few dates, we'll pay the kid's expenses along with yours. Some of us might even go as far as buying a pair of tennis shoes for the kid, when you drop that oh-so-subtle hint—"Look at my child's tennis shoes. He tears through those things like they're made of paper. I have to get him another pair already."

Many of us will pay the price of dating a woman with a child, and we'll pay for a while. Maybe a month, maybe a year, maybe only that first date when you bring your kid along.

Despite how much he adores you, there will come a time when your man will feel conflicted, wondering just what he is expected to pay for. He will wonder if his progress with you is directly tied to how willing he is to provide for your son or daughter.

And that's just for the first few months. There is the rest of that child's life your new man has to consider. Many families will decide to stop having children after two or three, because they simply cannot afford a larger family.

Many of us will not date women with children because we know that if we become close to you, and start a physical relationship with you, many of you will believe that, considering your child is a part of your life, and considering that you are providing for us in a number of ways, we should show appreciation and contribute to the upbringing of your child.

Despite the fact that your child is not ours, that your child may have a father who is present in his life and his voice will be heard in making decisions, and ours most likely will not, many of you still feel that men need to pay your child's way.

If the average guy were to give his opinion on this to another guy, 99 percent of the time he'd say this is ridiculous. If the average guy was on a date with a woman he was trying to get to know, and her eight-year-old daughter was brought along, he would dig in his pocket and do what he knew was expected of him.

But like I said before, if you abuse this sense of obligation that men feel, we will simply stop paying and decide that, even though you're a cool catch, it's much cheaper just taking out one person on a date, as opposed to two.

So in this situation, where you bring your child along on a date with the new guy you're dating, I advise that when it is time to buy those tickets, you have your child's ticket money ready. Most likely, the man will tell you to put it away, and that it's his pleasure to pay. Then again, some men will gladly take it, hoping to let you know exactly where he stands on the issue of financing children. He doesn't do it, and he never will.

Either way, the option should be given to the man, especially early on, when he barely knows you and couldn't pick your kid out of a small class of kindergartners. As time passes and he gets to know you and your child better, most likely he will take a bigger role in providing for your child. Then again, he may not. At that time, you will have a decision to make.

He might be a nice guy, but maybe he doesn't want to add your child to his list of expenses. In that case, you'll have to ask yourself, are you just looking for a nice man, or a nice man who's willing to spend his money on your child?

Fortunately, if you do decide to stick with him, and if the two of you marry, he'll be accepting a much greater responsibility for your child, and most men will do it proudly.

We know how important your child is to you, and rightfully so. You love your child, care for her, and provide for her. But there is one thing that you might not want to do:

Letting your kid make the decision

Now, men know it is important that before you decide we will be the one you choose for good, your kid will have to like us, get along with us. In other words, he will have to approve of us.

Does that mean he has the final decision?

It's bad enough he had to interview with you before you allowed us a second date. But now that the man you're interested in has impressed you, he has to do a song and dance for your kid.

Ladies, just so you know, men know when we're being set up for the kid interview.

"Little Timmy is having a birthday party," you tell your guy. "Would you like to come?"

He knows you want to see how he will interact with your child. And knowing that, your man will put on his best performance. He'll smile and be affectionate, and he might even bring the kid a gift.

But after the day at Chuck E. Cheese's, don't go home and ask your kid what he thought of your new friend, then base your future with this man on what your child says.

I know it sounds crazy, but some women actually do this.

He's your child. But why would you give him the power to influence a decision that may affect the rest of your life? The kid eats grass and still believes in the Easter Bunny.

Maybe I'm personalizing this, but I believe my failure with the woman I told you about earlier was based on what her pointy-headed kid thought of me. Kids want fun, silliness, someone who will let them act a fool, and be willing to act like one with them.

They want a clown, and if you allow your kid to go out into the world and bring you back a husband, an hour later, you'll find your child returning holding hands with Ronald McDonald.

Your six-year-old doesn't know what's best for you, so don't let the final decision rest with him.

I know, often kids may detect something negative in a man that you might miss. And if you truly believe there's something not quite right with the new guy, get rid of him. Don't pawn the responsibility off on your kid. Then again, if you were to leave the decision of whom you were going to end up with to your child, you might forever be alone. Most children will always want their natural father as opposed to the stranger you introduce them to, which can cause serious problems for your new guy.

Your baby's daddy

News flash! Your man wants to be the only man in your life, the only man you think of having any interaction with. Remember when you two first started dating and he wanted you to get rid of all your male friends? Remember when you went to social gatherings and he told you he didn't think it was appropriate for guys to give you hugs, or vice versa?

Men do that because we don't even want to think of the possibility of another guy getting some of what we feel is ours. And how about your sexual history?

Only the self-punishing glutton will want to know about the guys you were doing before you met him. Most of us will not even go there, because whether you've been with a hundred guys or one, we believe that what we don't know won't hurt us.

But what your guy, or the next guy you get with, does know for certain, especially after looking at that cute little daughter of yours, is that there definitely was another man, and you loved him, or were crazy enough about him to have sex with him. But not only that, you felt enough about him to carry his child and agree to raise her for the rest of your life.

And now we, as the new guy, step in, and of course we're going to ask, "So, is the father involved?"

Our fingers are crossed, hoping you'll say, "Naw. He fled the country and has sworn never to return."

Most often that is not the case.

A man feels he's lucky if you tell him that you haven't seen the father since the birth of your child. The father wants nothing to do with her, and you're cool with that. We don't mind hearing that, because at least we know that if we do get involved without the natural father in the picture, your kid won't have anyone to compare us to, and that makes the chances slimmer that we'll ever hear "You aren't my daddy, anyway!"

But many times, if you're a good woman and have a wonderful child, which I'm sure you do, the father of your child will most likely want to stay in his child's life, and that kind of poses a problem for the new guy.

I have a friend we'll call Steven. He has three children by three different women. He's never married any of them. But on the rare occasion he sees one of them, Steven makes an attempt to sleep with her. Whether they are in a committed relationship or not, Steven is shooting his game.

The sad thing is, none of these women have ever turned him down.

Steven believes, or should I say is sure of the fact, that because those women loved him once, and because he's given them children, and because they really wanted to be with him but he wouldn't grant them that, they will always want a piece of him.

"They love that kid, and whenever they look into his eyes they see me and realize they still love me."

That's what Steven thinks.

Is that true? Should men worry about you and your child's father? Maybe one night, after your kid's second birthday party, you'll have a few drinks together, reminisce about when the two of you were together, and end up having hot, sweaty, drunken sex as an attempt to bring back the past, if only for half an hour.

You say no, but we fear that. And we know we have reason to, because it happens so often.

A female friend of mine, let's call her Susie, told me she won't date a man who has a child younger than two years old, because she feels there would still be too much interaction between the father and the mother. Susie believes that things aren't sorted out enough between the two, even if they can't stand each other, because there is still the bond of that child, which came from having sex. This, in her opinion, could always land them back in bed together.

Why wouldn't men fear the same thing?

Especially considering that men know how other men think. We know how we feel about sex, and we know the father of your child might look at you, know that you have a new man, feel a bit of jealousy, and decide that he wants to see if he's still got it. He'll make a pass, tell you he still loves you and that he'll never cheat again, and what would be better than you and him making a go of it? You guys can be one big happy family again.

You wouldn't go for that? You'd honestly take the new guy you met six months ago over the father of your child? Most will think the opposite. That's why I'm providing a list of smart dating practices that will help the woman with children deal with the father of her child while trying to date:

- **If the guy you're dating doesn't ask about him, don't mention your child's father too often unless you have to.**

Guys have ridiculous egos. We want to feel as though it's all about us. We take offense if you speak too long about a guy at work who's doing a great job, because for whatever reason, we might think you have a thing for the guy at work and want to have sex with him. If you talk too much about your child's father we won't have to wonder if you at least *had* a thing for him and wanted to have sex with him—the child is the proof that you did.

- **Inform the new guy if he has no competition.**

If the father is out of the picture—if he's locked away, if he fled the country for Brazil, never to return, if he hates your guts, says the child is no way his and never wants to see you again, or if you just have no idea who the man is and don't care about ever finding out—

inform the new guy of this. This is information we like. This lets us know there will be no competition from the father, and we can comfortably fill that position if we choose. So even if the father is let out of prison on parole, or flies back from Brazil, you'll probably respect us more for taking on the responsibility of caring for your child than you would him for abandoning the little bugger in the first place.

- **Don't allow your child's father to have a key to your place.**

I know that's a tough one, especially if he helps a lot with the kid. And to tell you the truth, I'll take that one back. If he has a key already, no, you shouldn't go snatching it back because a new guy comes into your life. But don't tell your new guy the father has the key. Because of the relationship, most guys won't be shocked to find out that he does. What you should do is tell your child's father that he should use the key only after he okays it with you. You don't want your new guy to get up after sex, walk through the house naked to grab a glass of water, and find the father of your child kicking back in the living room, watching a game and having a beer. And trust me, babies' daddies will try that crap just to assert themselves as the man who first planted the flag on your behind.

- **Limit phone calls to only the essential ones.**

Nothing says there is something still going on like constant phone conversations with your child's father. And don't even bust yourselves out by having a special ring tone for that man. That way every time he calls, even if you ignore it, your new guy will know that it's him trying to contact you. Or if you pick up the phone while the two of you are out, then, after finding out it's your kid's father, you say, "Can I call you back, I'm in the middle of lunch," that's distracting.

What's really important is, if the father keeps the kid on the weekend or some weeknights, tell him to contact you only if it's necessary. You have to do this only before dates. But some fathers know that if they have the child, you're going to keep the phone at the ready, and will check it even if you think you heard it ring, just in case something serious happens. Some fathers are haters, and even though you're no longer with them because they cheated on you, and they are now about to marry the woman they cheated with, they don't want to see you going out and possibly getting to know a good man you might fall in love with. Don't let them sabotage a possible good thing by blowing up your phone while you're in the middle of a hot date with nonsense like, "Jason keeps asking for a Popsicle before bed. Do you think it's okay that I give him one?"

- **After you feel your relationship might be serious, inform your new guy of exactly what kind of situation you have with the father of your child.**

Some of you may consider what you've just read and possibly even practice it. Some of you may say the situation with your child's father is what it is, and if your guy can't handle it, then that's his business. That's respectable. But make your position known. If you believe that something serious could come from the situation you're in with the man you're seeing, sit him down. Discussing the depth of your relationship with your child's father could go a long way toward making that man feel more comfortable, and convince him that nothing is going on between the two of you.

Many of you believe we should just assume that if you're dating us, then there is nothing shady happening with any other man, let alone the father of your child. But imagine if the roles were reversed, and you were dating a man who had a four-year-old girl. His daughter was his heart. He could not stop talking about her, which meant that every now and then you got a news blast about the mother of that girl. You sensed that the man was faithful—he had given you no reason to believe otherwise—but one day he sat you down and said, "You obviously know what my situation is. I see my daughter at least two times a week, which means I see her mother, too. I just want you to know that although I did love her at one time, there is absolutely nothing going on between us now. She is a friend of mine and the mother of my child. When we speak on the phone, it pertains to our daughter. She's dating someone seriously now, who she's introduced me to, and one day, if you're cool with it, I'd like to have you two meet, just so you can put a face on the person I sometimes bring up, and you can also know that I'm serious about what's going on between us."

Wouldn't that make you feel so much more secure with that man?

When a man loves a woman

So you're involved with a man, and it's getting pretty serious. You think he might be considering proposing to you in the near future, and you know you'd accept, but there is that one little issue—your three hell-raising children. Will he accept a ready-made family when he doesn't have a single child of his own?

Just the other night, my friend said something that I thought was quite profound. It shocked me, actually, because normally the most profound thing he will say is something like, "It's always dark at nighttime."

Anyway, we were talking about women with children, and he said, "In order for me to love another woman's child, I have to love the woman first."

I'm going to ask you to read that once more, because even though it sounds pretty simple, there's much more going on there than it seems at first. This is the reason why you'll hear of a scandalous woman with five children, who has always been basically no good in your eyes, landing a great man. The man has no children of his own, but he happily agreed to step in and play father to her team of miscreants.

Why?

Because he loves that woman to death. He'd do anything for her. And because he knows she loves her children and he loves her, he wants to do what he can to show that love.

This explains why a man will, without hesitation, take responsibility for a woman's children. But what it also explains, in a very small way, is why so many men leave the mothers of their children, abandoning them.

If this statement—in order for a man to love a woman's children, he must love the woman first—is true, think about the men who have been married, fall out of love with their wives, and leave, only to pop up and take care of another woman and her children.

Now that I think about it, I had firsthand experience with that.

The woman my father left my mother for had a kid. I had seen him one time. He was a few years younger than me. I said nothing to him, just stared him in the face and knew that's where a lot of my father's attention was going.

But I also want you to think of the single mothers, and the men who never wanted marriage, the men who were never even in love with the women they were sleeping with. The woman gets pregnant, decides to give birth, and then what happens?

Of course, the woman is going to love the child because she carried it for nine months, because she brought the baby into the world. But how did the man feel? Where did he go? He left.

So many women expect the father to fall in love with the child just because she did, but unless he chooses to, he has no other investment than the fact that he contributed to the DNA of that child.

The baby arrives, and the man does not care for the woman any more than he had before she got pregnant, and he may even care for her less now because she may not have even considered whether or not he wanted the child. Now she expects that she and the man will be a happy family. But what happens next is that the man takes off, because he never loved the woman to begin with, so it's very likely that he will have no emotional ties to the child.

But I'm not talking about those guys. I'm talking about the man who loves you, the man who has decided he wants to marry you, and take responsibility for your children, because he knows how much they mean to you, and he will do anything to make you happy.

Is there any fear in his mind, anything that might make him

reconsider marrying you, due to the fact that you have those children? Yes, there is. And it's five little words:

"You're not my daddy anyway!"

Men fear having children. Whether out of wedlock or even if they're married and have been trying to get their wives pregnant for months, there is fear. We wonder if we will be good fathers, if we can teach the boy or girl everything he or she needs to know to go out into the world and be a success. But we not only fear that, we're scared of the responsibility we will have to accept, the changes the child will force us to make in our lives. Some of us aren't ready to make that kind of sacrifice, even for our own children.

Try to remember the time you told your man that you were pregnant with his child. Some of you remember that look of shock and horror and illness on his face. Remember all that fast talking he was doing, trying to convince you to get it taken care of? That was his fear talking.

He was told what it would be like to have to raise a child when he wasn't ready. He was informed of how difficult it would be. How his chief concern could no longer be himself but that child. He could no longer hang out and do what he wanted to do, but he would have to make money for that child, be responsible, set the right example.

Men fear being forced to make those kinds of changes in their lives. That's why, to avoid dealing with that, they do one of three things. Some put forth their most stringent effort never to get a woman pregnant before they are ready to have a child. But, if the man was careless, he will all of a sudden become the most persuasive man you've ever heard—bargain and deal, do anything, to get you to "take care of it." Or last, and what seems most popular, after the child is born, he'll just take off, run for his life.

Women with children, what you need to understand is, if a man is running away from his own children, if he is trying to cheat his kids out of child support, what makes you think he's going to take a look at your little one and decide to strive for father of the year? Why would he all of a sudden want to start forking over a percentage of his check toward *your* child's college fund?

It's not by chance that a man in his thirties does not have children. And in most cases, if he wants to have children, he wants to have some of his own.

So, to be honest, one of the main reasons we fear the woman with children is because, as in the example I mentioned earlier, it's not just about whether you are attracted to us and how you feel about us, but also because you expect us to win the approval of your child as well.

And yes, that makes sense. But for the average man who finds it hard enough just to keep a good relationship going with you, forcing him to jump through the hoops of satisfying your kids might just be too much for him.

But let's say the man is open to dating a woman with a kid or two. If we have a choice, we'd prefer those children to be little girls rather than boys.

Why? you ask.

We don't want to be yanked out of our homes and carted away by the police in handcuffs after we beat your son's behind because the little sixteen-year-old knucklehead thought he was big enough to try us.

I'm not saying that your new man can't marry you, and your kids can't fall head over heels in love with him, and everything can't turn out just fine, because it can.

But men will always at least consider the worst happening. We know there will be days when your kids will not like us, when we may have to exercise authority over them. On those days, they may even hate us.

That's when all the "You're not my daddy anyway!" nonsense comes out.

We hate that. We're paying bills, buying your kids shoes, and clothes, and food, and whatever else they need, but when we tell them they're grounded for smoking weed, we aren't really their father anymore?

If a man gets this from your daughter, he'll ask her to sit down so they can talk, or instead, he'll tell her to go to her room, because he doesn't want to say another thing about it. Either way, she's going to listen, because this man is at least filling the father role, and what girl ever tests her father? Yeah, she may scream, call him a name, slam a door to underscore how angry she is. But what girl *really* tests her father?

Many men are told by their grandfathers, or fathers, uncles, or brothers, that if you have sons, one day they will test you. Yeah, they're going to be your little pal, your little fishing buddy when they're kids, but there will be times when the man will have to pun-ish those boys, ground them, maybe spank them, and sometimes those boys won't forget that.

So at thirteen years old, after you've just grounded him, or whupped his behind, he'll sit in his bedroom, sulking, telling him-self, "When I get a little older, I'll show him he can't do that to me anymore."

Come sixteen or seventeen years old, he's found three chest hairs, along with the little bit of fuzz above his lip, and now he thinks he's a man and can set things straight with his father. What most men know is that if our biological sons would try us, there is a strong possibility it may happen with your son, who may not like, or never have liked, us.

Men who already have children won't shy away as much. They understand that if they're bringing children from another union to the table, they should not demand that the woman they are consid-ering dating be childless. But for some single men, the preference is not to have to deal with whatever drama may come from another man's child.

Your kid hates him: "You're not my daddy!" (Part 2)

So the man you're about to marry has accepted your son. Every-thing seems wonderful, but that man is thinking. He's proceeding cautiously, because he has questions. He likes your son, who is only twelve now, but he's wondering what will happen when your son turns fifteen, then sixteen, then seventeen.

Many men wonder what will happen when the child of the woman we're considering marrying finally decides to step so far out of line with us that we will need to punish him, get a little physical with him.

Will you allow that to happen?

You might say that your guy can punish your boy, but putting his hands on the child, whupping him, is something entirely different.

Let me tell you right now, that will cause a problem for most men; that is, unless you just don't believe in spankings. If you spank your child, and you allow the father of your child to spank him, but you just don't want your new husband spanking that bad little boy, then your husband will have an issue.

He will question the situation, asking himself why even though he is the man of the house, quite possibly his own house, and he is caring for your child like his own, paying for food, clothing, and whatever else he's agreed to pay for, he still can't punish your child.

Any man would feel offended if, although the child's biological father didn't want to marry you, and didn't want full-time responsibility of his own child, he still received some rights and privileges that he, your husband, did not.

So what do you do?

There's only one thing you can do. If the boy or the girl is bad, and it's common practice to spank in those situations, then if your new husband feels like doing the deed, you have to let him do it.

But what if you don't want to do that? What will happen?

Then you've tied your man's hands. In other words, you've made him powerless, a punk, and your child will read that, and take advantage of it. Why are most kids afraid of their fathers? Because their fathers are big, and they have deep voices, and most dads don't make idle threats.

Children recognize this and fathers usually don't have to spank children. A harsh verbal reprimand is enough.

But if your kid just accidentally dropped your husband's wrist-watch in the toilet, but your child knows that the man can't touch him because you forbade it, your kid just might walk up to him, spread his arms as if inviting confrontation, and coolly say, "So, what you wanna do about it?"

No, I don't think exactly that will happen, but your child will not feel threatened in the least by him. And no, your kid should not be scared of your man, but he should feel as though there are definite consequences to pay if he gets crazy.

But let's say that because you know your man isn't a child abuser, doesn't get a kick out of making babies or cute animals hurt for the fun of it, you give him the okay to spank your child if the child does something unforgivable. What do you suppose your kid might say the first time your man whacks him across his behind, or tells him to go to his room because he's on punishment?

"You can't do that," the child might protest.

"And why not?" most men will ask, just to see if the little snot has the nerve to say what he's thinking.

" 'Cause you aren't my daddy!"

And there they are, the words that men who date women with children always fear hearing.

Talk about a slap in the face.

Ladies, if you marry a man who is not the biological father of your children, before he moves in, or if he's already been living with you but your child hasn't slipped up and belched these evil words, pull them aside, and order, beg, or convince them never to say those words to the man of the house.

Let me tell you how that makes your man feel. After he's moved in with you, or accepted you and your child into his home, basically adopting him, agreeing to care for the child if he becomes sick or injured, agreeing to raise him, teach him, clothe him, and feed him, the man also makes an agreement with himself that it's okay to become emotionally attached to your child, that he can love him. Men do those things not because they have to, but because they want to. They agree to love your child, because they love you.

And when we do a good job at caring for your child, we'll take pride in that. We'll feel as though everyone is benefitting from our efforts. You're now getting help with your child, the child is gaining a father figure, someone to give him guidance and love, and, as the man, we're getting your appreciation for being there for your child.

But when your kid says something like, "You aren't my daddy anyway," all that pride and love that your man thought he was getting is wiped away.

Chapter Four

Fear of the Unknown

Baby weight

I know you've heard this a zillion times: men are visual creatures. Usually, we are first attracted by your physical appearance, and then, only after getting to know you, we fall in love with your brilliance, winning personality, and limitless compassion.

What beauty is, I don't know. I'm not one to believe that there is a standard in that area. There is no clear-cut, objective definition of the word *beauty*. It's in the eye of the beholder, right?

What one man considers beautiful, another man might consider grotesque. And a woman one man considers fat, another man might consider bony as all get-out. So, we as men love attractive women, meaning women we individually are attracted to.

Let's say you're a size 12. Your man likes your body, but regarding marriage, he's a bit concerned. Why? Because you haven't had children yet, and all men know that you gain weight during pregnancy, and that some women, despite how hard they try, can never shake it off. So what we do is try to factor just how much bigger we think you'll get after you have two or three kids, and then determine whether or not we'll be able to accept that.

Ugh! I know that really sounds bad. Shallow! Yeah, I know. I do really know, but I'm just telling you how it is.

We know you're doing us a favor by having our children. We

know that the pregnancy and birth thing does a job on the body that both you and your man love. But men remember the body of the woman he married, and if he has anything to say about that, he wants to see that body again.

This is one of the reasons why I say that a gym membership is so important.

Everyone should know that exercise can help you tailor your body, and can help you compensate for extra calories you might have taken in during the holidays, or that extra weight you just put on over time or because of pregnancy.

We know that a woman who works out would likely be quicker and more willing to lose weight than a woman who would just diet, or just started working out for the first time in an effort to lose pregnancy weight.

But even knowing that, men still will go to whatever measures we must in order to determine if you will gain the average weight most Americans do over time (1 pound a year), or if, after two babies and three years, you'll put on 125 pounds.

How do we do that?

Most men believe, whether it's true or not, that we can make a pretty accurate determination by sneaking a peek at your mother. "The fat-gene test" is what we call it. If your mother is overweight, then we tell ourselves there's a chance that you might have fallen off the same tree and will gain weight later in life as well. That is, unless you're into working out, something your mother may not have done.

What's sad is that no matter how men try to couch it, whenever we mention that we're concerned with a woman's weight, we sound shallow, simple, and selfish.

People don't consider all the obesity-related diseases that wobble hand in hand with weight gain. But forget all that. Shouldn't a man, or a woman, for that matter, be able to say she prefers someone who is not overweight without having to be criticized for it?

And yes, men do realize it's different if we're already married to a woman and she gains. But I'm not referring to those guys. What I'm telling you is that single men who might be on the fence about marriage can be toppled off and scared away by the possibility that you might gain serious pounds.

A friend of mine and I were eating lunch the other day. He spotted a guy with his wife and two kids at a table. After he stole a number of glances at them, I said, "What?"

"You see that guy's wife?" he asked.

"Yeah."

"See how she looks?"

She was a little frumpy, thick around the middle, obviously due to the two little boys running around the table.

"Okay," I said. "I see. So?"

My friend shoved another forkful of food into his mouth and said, "Would you do her?"

I glanced at the woman, and although I figured she was cute at one time, now she looked like a housewife and a mother. For a single guy, that's not necessarily a turn-on.

"No," I admitted.

"I wouldn't do her, either," my friend said. "When I get married, I need the kind of wife that other men would want to screw after she has my kids."

Although said in a crass way, I think that sums up a lot about how men feel. We marry you for so many reasons, but one of the very important ones is that we are physically attracted to you. And we assume that you're going to pretty much stay that way for the rest of your life, allowing us to always be attracted to you.

But is that realistic?

Of course not. To think that man sitting, eating lunch with his wife, was not attracted to her was probably the wrong assumption. There is a very good chance that he may be more attracted to her now than before she gained the weight, because of the children she gave him and the love they cultivated.

But how would single men know that could be the case?

How could single men who have never been married know that after marriage, despite however many pounds you or your wife may gain, your love and attraction will grow?

We simply could not know, and that's why we base our opinion on what we see, what we want now as a single guy for the rest of our lives.

If we married you at size 12, we'd love you to stay there, but we aren't crazy. We like good cooking. We're going to gain weight and expect you to gain some right along with us. Just try not to outweigh us. And when we go to the gym, come with us, or, if you'd prefer, ask us to come with you on your walks or bike rides.

Just because we're attracted to you physically doesn't make us shallow, and doesn't make us selfish to the core.

Sex—quality *and* quantity

Sex is a major consideration for men when we think about marriage. We like consistency, and if we're giving thought to a particular woman regarding marriage, it goes without saying that we are getting good, if not great, frequent sex from her.

What men fear is what we so often hear from many of our male friends. If you only knew how many times we've been warned that the number of times we have sex with our girlfriends will fall off dramatically once they become our wives.

Yes, it only makes sense. We understand that sex with you might still be new right after marriage. We understand that after time, things will dull some. We also understand that once children are born, time for sex is lessened, obligations increase, careers may alter some things, along with a whole host of other changes.

We understand that. We just don't care.

At least not as single men thinking about how much sex we should receive as married men.

After we're actually in the situation, experiencing it, dealing with all the factors that can interfere with sex, sure, we'll sympathize then. But no man wants to hear, before he's even married, that the frequency at which he has sex with his wife will diminish.

That's like a car salesman telling his customer before he actually buys the car that after the purchase, the frequency at which his automobile runs will decrease.

Getting sex as a single man whenever we want it, then getting married and getting it only on occasion, doesn't sound like a fair trade to most men. Men who are thirty or thirty-five become accustomed to a certain amount of sex. Many men fear walking down the aisle because, if what so many of us hear is true, the quantity of sex we're having will drop off. But that's not all we're concerned about. There is also the issue of quality.

This leads me to another point that may halt men from proposing.

Is the sex you're giving your guy good? "Sure!" you confidently boast. But do you know that's the case? Did he propose after the first time he experienced sex with you? Oh. Then it's not really *that* good. But, then again, whose is? And we don't expect it to be *that* good anyway.

What you should at least know when having sex with your guy, the guy you could possibly see as your future husband, is that he has set a bar that you must clear, a level of expectation he's waiting to see if you can meet.

No pressure, though.

That bar represents only the best sex he's ever had with any of his past girlfriends.

Let me tell you how this works.

Everyone—men and women—have had past relationships with partners who have given them mind-blowing, heart-thumping, limb-numbing sex. But you didn't marry those guys, and we didn't marry those women. Maybe because they just weren't right for you. Or maybe we didn't want them because even though the sex was so great that we wanted to tell the world, including our mothers, about it, those girls, whoever they were, were lacking in other areas.

Let's say they didn't cook, or they nagged us to death, or any other reasons that men consider deal breakers regarding marriage.

So we walked away from those women. But it's not as though the great sex we had with a particular girl did not leave an impression on us. On the contrary. We never forget how wonderful, how delightful, the experiences were with that woman. So we file them away as a comparison test for future women.

This is your litmus test.

So if that woman gave your man eyes-rolling-to-the-back-of-his-head oral sex, then sister, in his mind, you need to be providing the same.

If she was a gymnast and could do a spectacular floor routine — vault onto the chest of drawers, then perform a double-back-flip dismount onto his penis, that man will at least be expecting you to do a cartwheel or two.

The fact is, no man wants to marry a woman who has been a slut all her life; we just want a woman who knows as much as a slut does.

No. Just kidding. Well . . . maybe not.

How we see it is, we've been having sex for fifteen, twenty years, and so have you. There's a certain amount you need to know, and know it well. We know that you have no problem telling a man you're having sex with what to do, where it should go, and how long it should go there if he's not performing to your expectations.

We don't want to do that. We're not going to do that. We

would sit in pain, grit our teeth, tough out the bad experience, then never call you back rather than say, "Uh . . . uh . . . biting is not good. No need for teeth. You aren't supposed to eat that, honey."

Fortunately for you, most men aren't so hooked on sex that we'll walk away from a great woman just because she can't outdo the girl in our past who gave us the best sex of our lives.

So, even though that girl had us coming back like a crack addict, there is the fact that she may actually have been using crack.

That's usually a deal breaker for the average guy.

You, on the other hand, don't use crack. We take that into account, and will knock off a little on the expectation test, meaning you won't have to score as high.

If you're smarter, nicer-looking, have a better job, make more money, are funnier, or a better cook, we will continue to compensate you for those things, understanding that, no, you'll never be able to do what she did sexually, but you did just win the Pulitzer Prize. We figure that should count for something. Unfortunately, we are still men, so it doesn't count for everything.

So, if you're a talented, smart, caring woman with whom your boyfriend has already had sex several times, and seems to have enjoyed it, then you should rest assured that if you're not as good as the girl who gave him his best sex, in addition to all your other qualities, you're damn good enough to keep him interested.

Now that you've gotten that far, let me tell you what will have him rethinking the idea he had of one day marrying you.

I know this may sound chauvinistic, but if there is one thing you should never deny your boyfriend of, it is sex. Men simply think there is just no reason to do that.

If he's taken you out to dinner, or if he's washed your car, or if the two of you just watched a movie and knocked off a frozen pizza, or even if he just woke up and wants some, when we roll over, tap you on the shoulder, and ask, "Honey, may I?" we expect you to say, "Of course you may," or just silently roll over while lifting up your nightgown.

I know, I know. What if you don't feel like it? You're more than a machine for sex, and you have a brain, too. Of course you do. And your guy loves you for all that. But if you are his girlfriend, and he's been dating you for a year, that means he's probably crazy about you. And if he's even close to thirty years old, the idea of marrying you has probably scrambled across his brain at least once.

But, on this one morning, at 5:36 A.M., when he was particularly in need of some of you, you told him no. How were you to know that the dream he just woke up from was of you and him walking down the aisle after being wed. How could you know that he might have been ready to pop the question after you gave him an early morning shot? You couldn't.

What I'm trying to say is, as a girlfriend who loves her boyfriend, you should know that we place an irrationally high value on sex. It's one of the reasons we introduced ourselves to you, took you out to dinner, started dating you, and, for us, one of the reasons we will marry you.

If you deny your guy sex, it will only have him thinking that may be a glimpse of things to come. This might sound ridiculous to you, but this is how we truly think.

Divorcing you

If there is one thing that you can be certain scares men out of their socks, it is divorce. With the horror stories that we have heard, seen on the news, and read in the papers about some woman taking her man for half of everything he owns in a divorce settlement—yes, men are very afraid.

Sure, most of those men in the news are very, very wealthy, and the average man makes about fifty grand a year, so why should the average man worry? you ask.

If a man with fifty million gets taken for half of his money, he's still a millionaire. If the average man gets taken for half, he's practically broke.

The point I'm trying to make is, this fear is on all men's minds. I know men who've had their future wives sign prenups, and they didn't even make six figures a year.

For some of you wealthier women, you chuckle and say a hundred-thousand-dollar annual salary should not require a woman to sign a prenup. But when that's all a man has, he doesn't want half of it walking away just because the woman he married decides after four years of marriage that he snores too loudly, or that she could have a happier life with her personal trainer.

Who gets the house?
Who always gets the house?

Okay, this is not to say that I'm not happy that after a divorce the woman is the one who most often gets the house. If that wasn't the rule, I, my mother, and my siblings would've been on the street or in a one-bedroom apartment after my parents were divorced. But I will say that if I was the one getting divorced, I think I would've wanted to keep my house. I would've kept the kids, and my wife could've left. But how often does that happen? How often does the man even get the choice?

Even if a man argues for that arrangement in court, and both parents are equally qualified to provide for and care for and love those children, the decision seems always to be made in favor of the mother. Men know that going in. And we've seen and heard too many times from friends and family members alike that the women they divorced got the house in the settlement.

I have a friend who was recently divorced. His wife got the brand-new house he just built from the ground up, and he got his stereo set.

Yeah, yeah, there's more to it than that. But when it comes down to it, the woman has a nice place to live, while the man has something he can play his CDs on.

Get yo' hand out my pocket!

Alimony. What is alimony? Believe it or not, most men really could not correctly define this word, but it still scares the living daylights out of them.

Alimony: an allowance paid to a person by that person's spouse or former spouse for maintenance, granted by a court upon a legal separation or a divorce while action is pending.

The definition states "spouse." It doesn't specify "man" or "husband," but generally, it's the man who pays alimony.

Okay, there are a few exceptions. Britney Spears's husband gets alimony. Terry McMillan's husband got some money. But, then again, most men don't marry women who make insane sums of money like that.

Most men don't marry women who make more than them, despite what you might believe.

So, as children, if men listen to their parents, eat their breakfast in the mornings and veggies with every meal, do well in school, go to college and grad school, find decent employment, make money, buy a house, secure investments, marry—we think we're set for life.

And then our marriage goes down the crapper.

So we've failed at marriage, which for many men is a big enough hit already. But it's almost too much to bear when after that a judge forces us to pay money to the woman who no longer cares to be married to us.

Ladies, you do understand why this frightens us, right?

I know this is the reason why women always want to marry men who make more than they do, or at least not much less. After all the hard work you've put into getting where you are, you don't want to pay some man a portion of your salary just because you weren't happy with him after you got married.

We feel the same way.

But then you factor in child support, placing the man in a situation where he probably wouldn't even want the house if he had a choice, because with everything he's paying for, he probably could no longer afford to pay the mortgage.

Those are my kids, too!

What's up with the so-called "visitation rights"? After you divorce your husband, are his kids now in prison, and he has to get permission to come see them? Since he was partly responsible for bringing them into the world, doesn't he already have the right to come see them and take them out for ice cream without clearing it with you first?

If he were still married to you, he wouldn't have to do that.

But now that you're divorced, has the husband somehow changed? After signing the divorce papers, has he become a threat to his own kids? Even the notion is absurd. But men fear this, and are horrified by it.

For the men who know they will have close relationships with their kids, they fear being played with.

Say, one Monday night, after watching a football game with the guys, on his drive home, he decides he wants to see his kids. He stops by your house—the house that used to be his house, too—and rings the doorbell.

You come to the door, looking surprised to see him, and say, "What are you doing here?"

He says, "Well . . . I want to see my son."

You say, "Don't you think it's kind of late?"

And he thinks, if he was still married to you, if he still lived in that house, no time would ever be too late. So now what's the deal?

"Can I please just see little Bobby," he says.

And then you say something like, "You know the judge said you get him every other weekend, and during the summer."

Oh, no, you didn't!

A man worries that just because his life has changed with you, you'll force his life to change with his children. We can't even handle the thought of that.

But here's something else we have to concern ourselves with. When your ex-husband knocked on your door that Monday night, what if when you opened it, he peeked in and saw some guy sitting on the sofa?

This is the guy you started dating after your divorce. The guy who loves you so much, he wants to marry you now, and would even adopt your children if your ex-husband wasn't still coming around. But since he can't do that, he vows to be the best father in the world to your kids, as though they didn't already have a dad.

So now there's some new guy trying to play father to your kids, confusing them, telling them not to listen to what their biological father told them, and trying to win some of the kids' affection over from their father. But as though that's not enough for men to worry about, there is still yet another fear men contend with regarding marriage:

The unfaithful woman

There's a saying: Men cheat more, but women cheat better.

Men don't like this expression. Ask some men, and they don't believe that women cheat. Ask others, and they'll say that some of you cheat, but most don't. Ask even more men, and they'll say that you cheat as much as men, if not more, and that you can never put anything past a woman.

Okay, the smart man knows that anything is possible—especially in a relationship. But most men believe that once he is married, there is no way—there better not be a way—his wife will cheat on him.

Why in the world would you marry us if you wanted to cheat?

This is one of the things we fear most about getting married. We know it's not always the case, but after you marry us, we believe we should be the only man in your life, the only man who can turn you on, the only shoulder you can cry on. You aren't supposed to look at, fantasize, or even dream about another man.

Women's night out

We understand why this is a ritual of single women. You ladies want to get dressed up, travel in a pack to a bar or a club looking beautiful, and pretend that you're there not to be seen, not to be approached by men, but because you just want to hear some music and dance.

Yeah, we buy that.

But some married women still participate in the sacred "women's night out" events. And to tell you the truth, men have no clue as to what that could entail. Women's night out could actually be "woman's night off" from being a wife.

On these nights, women could meet up at some restaurant, make sure you're not being followed, then splinter off and head over to whatever hotels you're meeting your side men at.

Of course, husbands don't believe that, because they trust you. They wouldn't have married you if they didn't. But men who aren't married yet—the guy you're dating and hope one day will marry you—isn't sure.

Why? Because not only do you still do "women's night out," you still do the "women's trip."

Oh, and if you didn't know, this is far worse.

What does a man think about his woman getting with five or six of her girlfriends, two of which he knows are downright sluts, and planning a trip to Las Vegas for the NBA All-Star weekend?

Why would his woman want to go there when the only attraction will be NBA players and thousands of wild men and women looking to hook up for nameless, meaningless, drunken sex? He knows it's not because she enjoys basketball, because he can never get her to watch even a single game with him. So what are we supposed to think? She must be going down there for the sex. At least that's what some men will tell themselves.

What's behind it?

Boy, if only we knew what drove some women to cheat on their husbands, then we'd know not to do X, Y, or Z. Even if some of your reasons were rational, we would be better prepared to stop your infidelity from happening.

But some of you just might cheat on your husbands because one morning you weren't feeling particularly good about yourself, you weren't feeling beautiful. You really needed your husband to tell you that you were indeed the most gorgeous woman in the world. He didn't. But that guy Stan from accounting who had been trying to get with you for the last six months said, "Wow, you really look lovely today."

Next thing you knew, at lunchtime you were in the janitor's closet kissing Stan while he unfastened your bra.

It might not be that cut-and-dried; then again, it might be.

That's what gives men the creeps. We marry you because we love you. And because you married us, we know you feel the same. We aren't stupid. Most of us know that marriage isn't perfect, and neither are we, nor are you. There will be problems. There might be a day or two that we go without speaking. We might do something stupid that has you avoiding us in the kitchen, and making a point of returning home only after you know we've gone to sleep.

But despite those issues, we trust that before you go out there and do something crazy, you'll come to us first.

But you're thinking that you can't take another day of not speaking. You need some interaction, and you know that your male friend John is always there for good conversation.

But you didn't know that John has always been such a good male friend because he believed that things would eventually blow up between you and your husband, and his day would come.

We don't want our wives to cheat.

If you all only knew that for most men, this is the one, single thing that you can do that will have us never take you back. In our minds, it is the lowest, most unforgivable, destructive thing you can do to us, and any man in his right mind knows never to look past this.

I know, I know, you're saying men cheat, too.

Yes, we do, but that's different. It's not as bad, and there are times when you should actually take us back if you catch us doing that.

Okay, okay, okay! Hold on. There's a reason I said that. Just give me a minute to explain before you throw this book across the room.

Your cheating heart

Okay, you believe there is a double standard when it comes to cheating. Men think it's different when they do it, and that they should be forgiven. You think that if we should be forgiven, then so should you. Cheating is cheating.

But every man you ask will tell you that it's not the same. Why? That's simple. Because it's just not.

Seriously. I'll tell you why in a second, but first let me lay out a scenario and show you why men have such an issue with the potential of his wife cheating.

Your man loves you. He marries you. He spends his time with you, tries his best to care for you, and you and he plan a future together. During this time, it's not all roses and chocolate candy. You two argue. He deals with your attitude. You deal with his stubbornness.

You have it out sometimes. Then, other times, you have the best times of your life.

Then while you're out alone with your friends, some guy at the mall catches your eye. He comes over smiling, saying all the right things, and your girlfriend is next to you, giggling like she's twelve again.

He hands you his card, and says he just wants to be friends, and that you should call him.

One night, after one of the worst arguments you and your husband ever had, he leaves to go to a bar, have a few drinks, and let off some steam. When you're sure he's gone, you call the man you met at the mall.

He's smoother now, has you tingling over the phone, talking dirty to you, the way your husband used to way back when. Now while you and your husband cook dinner, while you eat, even during sex, all you can do is think about this new guy.

You share a dozen more phone calls, which makes him feel like an old friend. You make a plan to meet at a hotel, not just to talk but to have sex. And you tell yourself that if he can do half the things he's bragged about, this little trip will be worth risking your life for.

You go, and you have a wonderful time. The sex is great, he's a perfect gentleman, and before you leave, you ask when you can see him again.

He tells you Wednesday.

So Wednesday is the day, and you see him on that day for the next three months, always packing a bag, always wearing new underwear, smelling sweet. You purchase special items just for him, keep all that stuff in the trunk of your car.

You still have sex with your husband, but it's married sex, missionary position, lights off, TV on, eyes closed. But what you have with your side man is wild, swinging-from-the-ceiling, tied-to-the-headboard, lights-on, radio-blaring-to-cover-the-screaming sex.

Your side man goes out of town for a week. He misses your Wednesday appointment. You're pissed, a little irritable. You take it out on your husband. He keeps changing the channel, and you scream at him, "Can you just turn to one station and leave it there. Jeez!"

He looks at you, wondering what's crawled up your butt, not realizing you're pissed because of what's not crawling up your butt.

Ladies, do you see what's going on here?

Your husband married you. He loves you. So much that he's willing to put up with all the noise and nonsense that often comes with that marriage.

He accompanies you to the mall, stands around like a six-year-old looking for his mommy while you shop for new sandals. He deals with nights when you "have a headache" and he's really in the mood.

But your side guy gets only the best of you.

He sees the new thong and bra set you just tore the tag off while you sleep in checkered, flannel, ankle-length nightgowns with your husband.

You give your side guy several different forms of sex, while your husband gets just enough to shut him up.

If you don't know why you're doing all this for the side man, I'll tell you. It's because you've fallen in love. Maybe not true love, maybe more infatuation, but there are definitely some strings connected to your heart now.

This is why a husband cheating is different from his wife's infidelity.

I'll explain more.

Wives often cheat because they are dissatisfied with something in their marriage. They go out and find a man to fill the void, whatever that void may be. When that man successfully does fill that hole, the woman is grateful, and develops an affection for him.

Most husbands, on the other hand, cheat simply because they are cheaters. Everything may be going great in their lives, in their marriages, but one day they wake up in bed and think, hmm, this would be a great day for some sex with a different woman.

So with no void to fill other than him wanting to commit a physical act with a woman he doesn't know, he sets out to get this.

The woman he seeks doesn't have to be smart, or affectionate, or compassionate. She just has to look halfway decent, and be willing to open her legs.

When she does this for him, he does what he's supposed to do, and the deal is done.

Your husband might agree to see her again, but it's for the same thing. The only reason why their meeting lasts a minute longer than it takes to have sex is generally because the woman won't be cool with him jumping out of bed, washing himself off on the curtain, then high scrambling out of there.

When your husband gets home, he doesn't think about this woman, doesn't fantasize about her. For the most part it's over, until the next time.

Are you seeing the point I'm trying to make yet?

Okay, getting back to you. You finally get busted cheating. Your husband is losing his mind, crying, and throwing things across the room, yelling, saying things will never be the same.

Why? Because you cut him deeply like no one ever could.

And that is because you may fool yourself into thinking that you were just having sex, but it was more than that.

After your husband found out, he immediately asked how long it's been going on. You told him six months, and that's when he really lost it.

He knows that every man out there who sleeps with a married woman does his best to impress her, to give her the best sex she's ever had. That guy knew he was competing with your husband, and he wanted to win, wanted to keep you coming back.

Why? you ask.

Because you're easy. And what I mean by that is, he doesn't have to deal with all the stuff your husband has to deal with. That's why that other guy is trying to impress you.

What your husband knows is that if you've been seeing him for that long of a period of time, he *has* impressed you.

If that man makes love to you the right way, you start to develop feelings for him. It might be love, it might not be, but while he's up there, looking down into your eyes, or sweating into your eyes, you're definitely experiencing the warm fuzzies, and your husband can't take that. He sees it as you being in love with another man, and for us, that is the biggest blow you could ever deal us.

Now it's your husband's turn. When he gets caught cheating, I always say the first question out of the wise woman's mouth will be a tearful "Do you love her?" She will ask that because somehow she knows that a man can have sex with a woman for six months, a year, hell, ten years, and not care a thing for her.

A man can be walking down the street and accidentally bump into a woman he's never seen before. She says to him, "Hey, want to have sex?" Most guys would look her up and down, and if she's attractive, he'll scan the street for a hotel and, after spotting one, grab her hand and yank her in that direction.

Unless a guy loves you, sex is just a physical act.

And remember, for guys, because there was no void, because he cheated just to cheat, there was nothing he was trying to fill.

That's why when so many side women ask the married man they're sleeping with if he'll leave his wife, he will laugh and may actually say to them, "Why would I leave her? She's my wife. I love her."

Now, don't get me wrong. I'm not validating a man cheating on his wife. I'm just letting you know how we see things, and why we fear the idea of it happening so much.

It really is because of the investment, emotional and otherwise.

We are taught to be tough, not to cry, to "be a man!"

We do that for most of our lives, then we'll find you and know that we can show that emotion, or even cry in your presence, and it'll be okay.

We can strip ourselves bare in front of you.

And then to find out that you've given to another man what we thought you could share only with us—most men will never forgive that.

CHAPTER FIVE

The Hesitant Man

Not all men are against marriage because they don't believe in it, or think it's a bad idea. Some men have not married yet, or fear the prospect of ever getting married, simply because they don't know if they're ready for the responsibilities that marriage entails. Because it's such an enormous, life-changing decision that we make when we agree to marry, without experience or knowledge of what could happen in the future, we often stand there on the edge of the cliff afraid to jump, believing that there will be nowhere to go but down.

The out clause — or lack thereof

The man you've been dating for a year and a half—the man you love—is staring at you. You look up from reading your magazine and catch him.

"What?" you ask, feeling a weirdness about his stare.

"Nothing," he says, staring at you a moment longer, then going back to his crossword puzzle.

What just happened?

He took a trip into the future and tried to see you there. He might not have told you, but he believes he might one day want to marry you, and since he told himself that he's been scared out of his mind.

When this happens, men will try to imagine the future you in their lives.

Will you be as cool as you are now, or will you become our mothers, and scream and yell until your head explodes? Will you shut off the "sex on" valve? Will you weigh a ton more than we do after you have a kid or two?

Men want to know these things. But of course there's no way of finding that out for certain. That's hard for us, considering that almost everything a man buys today comes with a money-back guarantee, or at least some kind of warranty—lifetime, limited, or at least a four-year minimum.

But with you—NO RETURNS, NO EXCHANGES!

When seeing a sign like that in a store, don't you just turn around and walk out, not trusting anything you'd purchase there? If the seller doesn't trust it enough to give you some kind of piece of mind that it won't just fall apart, then why buy it?

This is not to say we view women as property. We don't. But what if things don't go as smoothly as we want them to? We've heard the horror stories. We've heard what it's like trying to get a divorce today, heard how the courts favor women in custody battles. Not that we're certain it would ever come to that.

Sure, marriage with you might be the best thing that ever happened to him. But it's a gamble.

That's not to say that men don't eventually propose. If we're thinking about it, and you're great for us, and the timing is right, we will eventually muster up the courage to ask for your hand.

But until then, know that we're sweating about the uncertain future, and panicking even more, because there is no easy out clause, just in case marriage with you is a nightmare.

No romance without finance

Ladies, even though you might not want to admit it, there are plenty of good men out there. Many of us were raised quite well. We were given a good example of what a man must do to succeed in love, taught how to prosper and make a decent living so we can provide for a wife and children when that time comes.

A lot of men are doing that, too. For so many of us, that is our chief motivation for working hard, for climbing the career ladder. We want everything in place so that when we finally meet that woman we want to marry, all we'll have to do is simply propose and move you in. You'll fit snuggly into our lives like a puzzle piece.

For men, there was a time when just any woman would do. She may have been cute, considerate, and caring, was willing to cook a meal and wash clothes, so the man making six figures would've gladly snatched her up.

Ladies, those men are dying out in droves.

As you well know, many women in the past, especially the cute ones, always felt they could use their good looks to land a good, well-paid man. Their mother may have told them that. Everyone, for that matter, may have told them that.

Beautiful women would not date ordinary guys because they felt they deserved better, based solely on the skin they were in. In high school—oh, she dated only basketball players, or football players, or guys who went to other schools who had cars.

Some of those beautiful women may have been so busy being beautiful that they did not spend much time doing schoolwork and planning a future, and, upon graduating, all they had to go with that high school diploma was their beauty.

Those women would have to cash in on a good, money-making man, and they would have to be fairly quick about it. Because the kind of man they were looking for, who was basically buying beauty, would much rather purchase young beauty than old beauty.

Back in those days, the well-established man who was CEO of some Fortune 500 company, or some professional ballplayer, or independently wealthy, would marry one of these women.

They would get her home, prop her on the sofa, and stand in awe of her beauty. And each day the man came home from work, his beautiful wife would be sitting there on the sofa, looking beautiful. And each day he left in the morning, she'd remain there looking just as lovely.

On occasion, she'd complain when things weren't right around the house, or when he didn't buy her the right diamond ring, or when he bought her the Mercedes CL instead of the SL.

Eventually, the man started looking at his financial situation and realized that the beautiful woman stationed on his sofa wasn't contributing much to the household, and added nothing to his bank account.

But while at work, he also realized that there were women there who worked just as hard as he did, held the same degrees that he held, and brought home as much money, if not more.

He scratched his head, as many men were probably doing at that same moment, while looking at his beautiful, sofa-sitting wife, and realized that maybe he could've chosen a bit more wisely.

What's good for the goose . . .

Whether beautiful or not, women always felt as though they should marry up. I'm sure I don't have to explain this term, because this was probably defined for most of you by your mothers and grand-mothers.

Truthfully, it only makes sense. Why shouldn't a woman want a man who is doing well, even better than she is? She should want that. It makes life easier. Twenty or thirty years ago, a millionaire could walk into McDonald's, see a beautiful woman cooking fries in a vat of popping-hot grease, ask her out, then marry her six months later.

But, like I said, that's quickly changing.

Men work hard for the few dollars we earn. And just like we aren't trying to spend a hundred bucks or better on a first date just for a thank-you and a firm handshake as you exit our car, we aren't trying to continue to pay our student loans for the rest of our lives only to marry a woman with no formal education and a spotty em-ployment history.

By now, everyone should know that one of the main causes for divorce is money. When there's not enough of it, folks get cranky, start laying blame, argue, and then the end approaches.

This is not to say that money will make a marriage a happy one. But a man knows that if money isn't an issue, that's one less thing he'll have to worry about destroying his union with his wife. So nowadays, a man looks at himself on paper. He realizes that his education, his title, his position, and his annual income give him status: good-catch status, I like to call it.

Because he has achieved this by working hard all his life, he's not going to be quick to lose it. We realize that one of the quickest ways to turn our entire lives around is by marrying. It could be for the better or for the worse, depending on the type of woman we choose.

Do you know what choosing the wrong woman can do to a man's salary? It can cut it in half. We are frightened of that. So now we've become pickier. And we can do that because of your success.

That's right, ladies. Because you've fought and struggled for equal rights, and equal pay, because there are as many, if not more, of you attending college than us now, it betters not only your situation but ours as well. No longer do we have to hope that we can convince our beautiful wife to go to work or take a class after we marry her. Now we are looking for a woman who has just as much as we do.

Even if we are the president of a successful company, we are looking for a woman who has the same or similar. If we are a coach at a local high school and we own our own home, then we want someone who has some of the same.

For the beautiful women who stare into the mirrors of their compacts all day, applying lipstick, take notes from the women who are rushing to class, or applying for that higher position. Those are the women men will be pursuing.

It's all about the money

One of my friends told me yesterday that the woman he is presently dating, who is making considerably more money than he is, told him that if they were to marry, the money that came into their home would belong to both of them.

If you made much more money than the man you were dating and told him that, you'd think that he would be grateful, that whatever worries or concerns regarding the fact that you double or triple his income would automatically disappear.

Well, that's not necessarily the case. Most men, whose sole intention isn't to marry you for your money, will thank you for that offer, but will not take you up on it.

Why? you ask.

Because despite how old-fashioned this may seem, men still feel it's our responsibility to be the breadwinners of the household.

You could make $200,000 a year, and we could make $20,000, but when you offer us some of your money, most men will say, "No, no, I'm all right," even if he has only ten dollars to last him until payday.

In taking money from you, we feel as though we're relinquishing some of our control, some of our manliness, and although you might be saying, "Oh, nonsense!" it's true, and you know it.

That's the reason why some men steer clear of women who make considerably more than they do, or have more assets. But I'll get to that in a later chapter. Back to the money issue.

As I said before, in being the man, claiming that we are the head of the household, we feel we have to be the breadwinner. In order to do that, we have to have a decent job, have our finances in order, and bring our debt down.

Unfortunately, this takes time for some men—that is, if it ever happens.

Becoming a success isn't as simple as it sounds. Many men don't accomplish what they had hoped once acquiring their degree, many more don't finish, and even more simply don't attend.

So as the average twenty-five-year-old guy still blows money on beer, rent, and accessories for his car, he tells himself he'll pull it together when he gets a little older. Thirty comes around, and he's stuck in the same dead-end gig he was working when he was five years younger. Only now he's serious and wants to excel, but that associate's degree from that junior college isn't the key to riches he thought it would be.

So at age thirty-five, when he desires marriage, he looks around and realizes he still lives in an apartment, is still waiting until next Friday for his paycheck so he can buy groceries and pay whatever he can on overdue utility bills.

Even if your guy's situation isn't this dire, even if he has little or no debt but is still living in an apartment, or has zero savings, he may look at himself whenever you mention marriage and think, "I'm barely making it on my own. How will I be able to support a family?"

So despite how much money you make, how much money you say you will contribute, if we aren't confident that we can provide for a family by ourselves, many of us won't even consider the prospect of marriage.

Workin' nine to five

Most men aren't independently wealthy. If you know such a man, marry him. Fast! Most of us work a nine-to-five and punch a clock, just like most of you. Considering that, many men know what it feels like to be let go from a job, or they know someone who does. That someone might have even been their father.

And what happens after that? Nothing good, let me tell you.

A lot of men consider what they do for a living a big part of who they are as individuals.

How many times have you been in a club, and after a man introduces himself, he sticks out his chest and tells you he's a doctor? Or maybe he's not that blatant, and while retrieving his cell phone he "accidentally" pulls his stethoscope out of his suit pocket and drops it on the floor at your feet.

He's a doctor first, and a man second. That's why he'll look at you like you just slapped his mama if you don't call him *Dr.* Taylor. That's why he has DOKTOR 3 on his license plates.

You get my point?

When a man works a gig, the money he makes is part of what makes him a man; it's what makes him feel he should be in control.

A forty-two-year-old friend of mine told me one of the reasons he's not married is because he's still living from check to check, and he's uncertain about the status of his job. If he were to marry, have a child, start buying stuff on credit, get a mortgage and a couple of car notes, all totaling just a few dollars under what he and his wife were to bring in per month, and then he lost his job—well, what in the world would he do then?

Men know that sometimes, despite how hard and long we check the classifieds, surf Monster and CareerBuilder, if the job gods don't want us to find employment, then we won't find it.

Meanwhile, we're sitting at home getting addicted to judge shows and talk shows, and our wives are telling us what losers we are. The last person we want to see us as losers is our wives. And trust me, a man feels like a loser long before his wife is finally fed up enough to define him as one. We don't want to see our children suffer and go without.

As the head of the household—there goes that self-proclaimed title again—it's our responsibility to make sure that does not happen. And if it does happen, something strange occurs—a reversal.

When a man is earning money and refusing to take money

from you because we tell you we're the man of the house, you say, "Oh, whatever. We both contribute to this house. There is no man of the house."

But when we lose our jobs, when the bills are late, or going unpaid, you look at us in disgust and say, "I can't believe you're letting this happen to us. You're supposed to be the man of the house and you can't even find a job."

Now, I know you think this isn't rational thinking, but, like I said, this is what we fear.

Many of us hesitate to marry because there's nothing wrong with us struggling alone. We'll eat cans of pork and beans and twenty-five-cent plastic bags of Ramen noodles until the cows come home. But not having a job, or not being certain that the job we are currently working will last, will definitely stop us from considering marriage.

Like father, like son

In the first novel I ever wrote, there is a character, the oldest son of three. His father left him and his two younger brothers when they were just children. Their father didn't speak to them again until twenty-five years later. At that time, this character, whose name is Austin Harris, was in the middle of leaving his wife and children.

I never really gave an explanation to the reader of why Austin wanted out of his marriage. Yeah, I had him argue with his wife, and he had a couple of gripes, like her not cooking dinner enough, but it was nothing that should've had him packing his bags.

I wanted the reader to feel as though maybe Austin was compelled to leave by something he wasn't even certain of, almost as if it were something hereditary—a gene passed down from father to son.

Believe it or not, some men fear that something similar to this actually happens. If their old man was rotten, worthless, a coward, and took off when his children were still rolling around on the floor in Pampers, some men fear they may do the same thing.

If their father was inattentive, or unemotional and not very affectionate, some men would rather not get married, not have children, than run the risk of finding out that they possess the same awful traits their father had, and later end up abandoning their families.

We having fun yet?

How many people do you know who have gotten married, and three short years later found themselves filing for divorce? How many couples do you know who have divorced after only half that time? After nine months? After six?

Everyone knows somebody like that. Men will ask themselves, why does that happen? If they were to ask their poor sap of a friend who was going through a bitter divorce, of course that man would say it was his wife's fault.

In a previous chapter, I mentioned that men fear you changing after marriage, which stops some of us from ever going through with it. This is not that. This is about men fearing that after we've been married, we just might wake up one day and realize we've made an awful mistake.

Ladies, let me tell you something you might not have already known. No man, including yours, will ever be as excited to get married as you will be.

I'm serious. So, so serious.

You're saying, "No, my man is different! Whenever I ask him if he's excited, he'll stop whatever he's doing, look at me a minute, then say, 'Yeah, baby. I'm excited.'"

Okay, well, if he's that excited, next time you guys are looking at invitations, or choosing color schemes for the wedding, without warning, quickly look at him. What you'll see is a man either on the verge of being so bored he's about to fall off to sleep or in so much pain that he's considering getting up, running out of that wedding boutique into traffic, and getting hit by a car. That would be painful, too, but at least he wouldn't have to choose between the pastel blue or the sunset red for his hospital bed sheets.

We say that we're excited about marriage because we know you want us to be excited about marriage. That's not to say we dread it. That's not to say we even dislike it. Most men who agree to marry want to marry. We like the idea of being married to you, but we agree to it not because we think it'd be so fun that we can't wait to start married life.

Men do it more because it's the wise thing to do.

Yes, we also do it because we love you. But we've loved many, many women, and we didn't marry any of them.

I hate to tell you this, but most men, at least the men who have entered that marrying age I've spoken so much about, make the decision to marry more with our heads than with our hearts.

Here's something sad that I was discussing with my brother one day not too long ago.

Men don't fall in love anymore. Well, we still fall in love, but not the way we used to when we were teenagers, or when we were in college, or even into early adulthood.

Back then, all there was to be concerned about was if we were attracted to a girl, and if she was a good, loving person. If she was, then we'd grow to like her, then love her, then feel as though we couldn't live without her. It was all about our feelings for her. Nothing else.

Today, since we've gotten older, lived in the world a bit longer, succeeded and suffered, we've learned there's more to life than just love. There's good credit and bad credit. There's debt and job history.

So when we meet a woman today, we might consider her because she's beautiful, and loving, and a wonderful person, but we'll never get to truly know her, or fall in love with her, because many of us will discount her the moment we find out she has five kids at home, by three different fathers. Or, upon first meeting another woman, we might think she is our soul mate, but we never return her phone calls after finding out she sells newspapers on the corner.

You say that's just another excuse not to have to commit to marriage. You believe we feel this way because we're just scared. That might be true, but it might not be.

I will admit that all men fear marriage, even just a little bit. Not necessarily in the way I've been talking about so far in this book, but in the way that anyone would fear walking down a dark tunnel, not knowing what's on the other side.

Older, wiser men will tell us younger men that it's something that just has to be done. That leap of faith. If we think too hard, we'll never jump. So many of us don't, because there's no guarantee of a soft landing, of a successful marriage. For that reason, we often think it's safer just to stay unmarried than to have to deal with being married and realizing after the fact that we no longer want it.

Still sowing oats

A man in his forties told me he wasn't getting married yet because he just hadn't gotten everything out of his system. He said he wasn't sure if he could count on himself not to cheat if he did marry.

Let me tell you, this is a huge one with us.

You probably don't know this, but unfortunately many men don't fear whether or not they'll be faithful to you once they marry you, because they are certain they won't be. Many men know they will cheat after marriage, because they've never been committed to just one woman in their lifetime.

To be honest, what should worry the man you're considering marrying is whether he'll get sick of having sex with just you, or you will with him. Considering marriage is supposed to be a monogamous union between two people for the rest of your lives, this should be a natural concern.

So, if you normally have open conversations with your guy that deal with sex and this hasn't come up, it's probably because he's not worried about getting bored sexually, considering he'll be supplementing you with other women.

It's a shame, but men will stand at the altar, shed a tear of joy or two, and as soon as your flight lands returning you home after your honeymoon, he'll call his girl on the side so they can reconnect.

The truth is, if we love you, we don't want to cheat on you. So some of us would rather not even risk marrying you, cheating on you, and getting caught, which we know we eventually will. All men eventually get caught. So many men see waiting until we're sure we're ready to marry, if we ever marry at all, as saving you and us the heartache and pain of our possible betrayal.

CHAPTER SIX

Always a Bridesmaid, Never a Bride

Although it might seem that way, not every woman has an issue finding a good man. Some of you make it harder than it has to be. It's not necessarily all your fault, but your beliefs, your actions, and simply your opinion of men could be the reasons that stop you from finding the man you are searching for.

Return the favor

What if every man needed to determine what a woman's annual salary was, what her house was worth, her position at work, and her level of education before he considered dating her?

And what if after finding out that she did not meet his qualifications, he determined that he could not date her? Do you know how many more women would never marry? Obviously, that is not the case with the majority of men.

Most men, if attracted to a woman, will consider her, regardless of what she does for a living, despite her level of education or where she lives. She could wash street signs for a living, be studying for that dreaded eighth-grade equivalency test, and live at home with her mother, father, and three little brothers. If she's cute and is a fun person, some man will at least consider her.

What's more, if we fall in love with her, we'll even marry her.

As stated in the previous chapter, as men, we feel it's our responsibility to be the head of the household, to care for our wives, to provide for them, make their lives better.

The guy who marries that woman might tell her, "Baby, you won't always have to clean street signs. Once you graduate from eighth grade, you can work your way up to windows, and maybe even doors."

For so many years, it was considered commonplace for the woman to stay at home, raise the children, and keep the house while the man worked to pay the bills. Of course, that's not to say that every woman wanted that situation. That's evident in how many of you work today, and run your own households.

But considering that we had no issue with it then, and taking into account, with only a few exceptions, that most men still are concerned first with whom you are as a woman, as opposed to how much money you rake in, won't you consider us the same way?

You, the intimidator

"He's just intimidated by you and your success," your girlfriend will tell you. This is often the excuse, or explanation, as to why you may have problems finding a good man.

We've all heard it before. That man you went on a couple of

great dates with finally comes to your house, and once he sees it, with its twelve bathrooms, circular driveway, and two acres of rolling hills, he cuts out of there as if his pants are on fire.

I've been told by my successful female friends that they know now not to disclose the fact that they own a home too soon, because that often intimidates men.

I've had the pleasure of being personally insulted by a woman I dated, when for quite some time she refused to tell me what she did for a living. When she finally told me and my eyes didn't balloon, my jaw didn't drop open in awe of the fact that she was a chemist of some sort or another, she did her best to make the work sound as prestigious and intriguing as possible.

Ladies, from now on, I don't believe you should feel that men are intimidated by you. But I think you should know that we are often impressed by you, and, quite honestly, because of everything you own, and have accomplished, some men might believe you just might be the wrong fit for them. Let me explain by giving you an example.

Another friend told me about a man she had dated a couple of times. On the third date, she had invited him to her house. But upon seeing it, he freaked out a little. He told her, ten minutes after sitting down on her sofa, inside her very nice house, "You know, maybe we should stop this right now. I don't think I'm the right guy for you."

He was spooked. But let's get it straight, that was not intimidation. That was a man trying to avoid putting himself in a place where he had no power, or less power, than the woman he was with.

Let me break it down this way. If points were given for experiences, assets, age, education, income, and job title, a man would tally these points to help him determine whether or not the woman he's considering is a woman with whom he could have a successful relationship.

I have a friend who was in a relationship that is now over. I was never fond of the woman, and I knew the relationship would end sooner or later. This was because in all the above categories, she had more points than he did. This woman was also older than him, which I'm sure made her believe she was wiser. She had more education, she made more money, her job was more prestigious, and what doomed the relationship from the start was the fact that he lived in her home.

The homeowner is the ruler. Period. It doesn't matter if it's the man or the woman.

Men understand that. Either they've experienced it or they know someone who has, but no man wants to be on the receiving end of his woman telling him, "If you don't like it, you can get out of *my* house."

My friend was walking on tiptoes, on eggshells, it seemed, the entire time he lived under her roof. This woman would fault him in front of company for not washing the dishes. I could tell he was not himself for fear of pissing her off and getting put out, which actually happened anyway.

I refer to this as the woman having the man wear panties. The woman takes on common male behavior, and the man becomes cautious, censors himself, and becomes more submissive.

Most men never want to find themselves in this position.

It's the reason why some men aren't interested in women they know have earned more points than them. A man living in an apartment will often avoid getting too serious with a woman who owns a nice house. One reason is because he knows that if the two of them go all the way, he will most likely be giving up his apartment to move into her house, putting him in the potential situation of wearing panties.

And that's why you find many men who have accomplished on the same level, or more than you, dating women with much less than they have. It puts us in the position where we can control, where we can say, "If you don't like it, you can get out of *my* house."

So, men truly aren't intimidated by what you have.

C'mon, ladies. What man wouldn't want to be elevated from living in a studio apartment to lounging in your big house, from driving his busted Hyundai to driving you around in your Benz? We avoid that not because we are intimidated by you, but because we fear that once we are in a relationship with you, you will become an intimidator.

Blame it on your mama

Some of you are walking around with a negative opinion of men, and you don't know why. This might help you to understand.

Remember earlier when I stated that young men and boys who have had bad experiences with their own fathers can be negatively influenced regarding marriage?

If a boy's father had a terrible experience in his marriage, most likely he wasn't the only one. His mother was probably having just as much of a rotten time, and couldn't wait until her husband finally packed all of his things and got out of there.

So, after the divorce, there's a chance that when the boy visited his father, the man would tell his son about the marriage, and that maybe he should wait, or not do it all, in an attempt to save his son some of the grief he went through.

But what if there was no little boy? What if there was just a little girl? And say that little girl was you. What if after your father walked out of the house he never came back and never had contact with you again?

That would most likely have left your mother in a position where not only was she unhappy with her husband during marriage, but she was also dissatisfied with him because he behaved like a trifling father.

Then it was just you and your mother. She raised you, fed you, and counseled you. And part of that counseling covered how to land you in a better place than where she was. How you could avoid the pitfalls she fell into. She did for you what the father sometimes will do for us.

Your mother may have told you that she wanted you to go to college, because she wanted you to have more education than she had. She wanted you to get a job so you could buy the things that you wanted, have the lifestyle you desired.

She told you those things because obviously she wanted the best for you. But regardless of whether she informed you of this or not, she was also telling you those things because she didn't want you to rely on a man.

Some mothers are more subtle than others. They may say, "I want you to have a good education and a good job, so when the time comes, if you want to buy a house and you're not married, you can do it."

Other mothers aren't as sweet about it. "You get a good job and make your own money so you can buy your own things, live your own life, and won't have to ask a man for nothing!"

It's bad enough that from the year your father left to the year you moved out, you probably heard negative comments about him, as well as the man, or men, your mother tried to replace him with. And if your mother wasn't the type to speak negatively about your father, then you may have witnessed some of the effects that divorce had on your mother.

Those things may have turned you off to marriage, just like they have to us.

But when you add to that your mother's influence, or even your father's, it might have you thinking twice about walking down the same path they did.

The training you didn't get

How many times have you seen this scenario? A little boy whacks his sister. Their mother swoops down out of nowhere, grabs the little boy by his shoulders, and shakes him so hard the bubble gum pops out of his mouth. "You don't hit your sister!" their mother screams.

"Boys don't hit girls. Do you hear me?" Shake, shake, shake. "Do you hear me?!"

Or the mother tells her son, "Open the door for your grandmother." Or, "Pull your seat out for your auntie." Or, "If you want to impress that girl, then buy her roses."

Because many of your mothers have been dogged by your fathers, they don't want your brothers—us—to grow up putting the future women in our lives—you—through that kind of drama. So what do many single mothers of today do? They teach their sons how to be good men. They try to teach them how to be honest, how not to cheat. They teach their boys what their potential future wives will like and won't like. In other words, they try to prepare their boys to be the most respectable men they can be. They're grooming them.

But while your mother is telling your brother that he should carry your bike up the stairs because that's what good boys do, is she telling you that you should go upstairs and fix your brother a sandwich because that's what good girls do? I seriously doubt it.

Now, I know, back in the days of our grandmothers and great-grandmothers, they would pass on knowledge to their daughters like, "Always fix the man's plate first, and then, when he's settled, you fix the children's plates, and then you can sit down to eat."

Generations ago, there used to be home economics classes in high school, where kids were taught how to care for the home, make a budget, cook, and clean. These classes were meant to educate young women on how to care for their husbands and their children. Along with that knowledge, the example the girls' mothers would set when taking care of their fathers would more than prepare the young women for marriage.

But now that the divorce rate is so high, because so many children never know their father, there is no longer that example. And since home economics classes are no longer taught in school, girls are no longer formally educated on how to care for the home.

So, while the mother of a boy and a girl knows what to tell her little boy—knows what women will expect, because she, herself, is a woman—she doesn't quite care about what to teach her little girl about keeping house, or caring for a man.

But without that knowledge, girls grow into women who can't clean a house properly or cook a balanced meal, and that's a shame. Not because all women should know how to do that, but because *everyone* should know how to do that.

My mother taught me how to clean the bathroom the correct way when I was eight years old. I looked at her like she was crazy when she brought the pail of soapy water in and told me I had to get on my hands and knees and scrub behind the toilet. But I did it, fearing a whupping, and I still do it to this day.

I know how to treat a woman, chiefly because my mother taught me how.

But the question that begs to be asked is, did your mother teach you how to treat a man? More important, are you teaching your daughter?

CHAPTER SEVEN

Women's National Anthem:
"I Don't Need a Man!"

You've said this before, haven't you? C'mon. That time when you were pissed off at your boyfriend, or when he told you he was done with the relationship and walked out on you. You've said it. Or at least you've thought it. And if you haven't, I know you have at least three girlfriends who have made that statement.

I know what saying those five words is supposed to do.

It's supposed to be empowering, right?

"I don't need a man. To hell with them! I can do bad all by myself. Ain't nothing going on but the rent. And you know it, girl-friend!" A few high-fives, a couple of sips from the apple martinis, and man-bashing night can continue.

But even if it is true, does it give you strength to say it?

Sometimes when speaking to groups, or while doing book signings, this discussion will come up. And although I've heard several women make that statement, I can say that I've never heard a man utter those words about women.

Why?

Because men need women, and we aren't afraid to admit it.

Most of what men do is because of women. You are what drives us to be successful. You're what motivates us to stay in shape, to appear smart and witty, to drive nice cars, to lower the toilet seat when we're finished.

In plain English, we love women. Why would we say we could live without you?

Now, I know what you're proclaiming when you say this, and technically it's true. Women don't need men to survive. You need us to procreate, or at least you need something from us to do that, but lately, some women pretend as though you can find a way around that, too.

I believe you're saying that if your man is going to take you through these changes, or start up with those issues—cheat on you, lie to you, try to lay his hands on you, and then have the nerve to ask if you have five hundred dollars—you don't need him. I agree. But I think you should be more specific. You don't need *that* guy. That one man who's been playing the fool. You don't want *him*. That doesn't mean there aren't other men out there who wouldn't be perfect for you.

But often, you don't take that approach. You may have been hurt, or you're bitter or resentful because your man left you with three kids, and now there's only so far you can go with your career while he's out who knows where chasing skirts. Or maybe you were fine with starting a family when he promised that he would be there to participate in that, but at the first sign of trouble, he's a ghost, and now you're wondering, did you ever really want a child, or did you do it for him?

Now every man is labeled a clown, or worthless. You carry that attitude around with you, and even when you're over the man who did you wrong, even when you're ready to try something with another guy, new guys can smell that attitude coming a mile away.

So what do they do? Rightfully, smartly, they head for the hills. Now you're asking, "Why can't I find a man?" Because you didn't need one, remember? So what do you do? Do you carry that attitude around with you for the rest of your life? All that will do is, like I said, have men running from you the moment they see you coming with that huge chip on your shoulder. What happens then?

The cycle starts.

You're looking to become involved again with another man, but because you're going into it lugging that baggage your last man saddled you with, a new man doesn't want anything to do with you. And when that happens, you become angry, frustrated, wondering why no man wants you. When you can't find the answer, or fail to realize it's because you might have a low opinion of all men, or you feel a man's only value to you is to fill an occasional sexual need or act as a date at a dinner party, you'll tell yourself you truly no longer need them.

We know that many of you scream those words because you've been hurt by us, and telling yourselves that you don't need us is like promising yourselves that you will never fall prey to the pain that we, as men, so often deliver to you. In other words, you're telling yourselves you'll never trust another man again, because that's where you get in trouble.

If you could actually do that and be happy with your life, you might make out better for it.

Believe it or not, men have been known to abuse the trust that women give us. That's just the type of men those guys are. But I want you to really think about some of the men you trusted, and what you trusted them with.

Even as you were writing him that check for ten thousand dollars, money that he said he would pay you back even though he was not employed, that little bird was fluttering around in your brain, screaming, "Don't do this!" Yet, you did it anyway. Why? Because you said you loved him, and made yourself believe you trusted him.

I believe that the main reason you feel mistreated by men is simply because they did you wrong. You were in what you thought was an honest, monogamous relationship for six years, only to find him in bed with another woman. No, you couldn't have seen that coming.

But yes, there were times, ladies, when you knew that the man you were with was no good. He had done you wrong a thousand times before, but you could never kick him to the curb, and the only reason you're free of him today is because he left you. And now you're angry, and screaming, "I don't need a man!" You are truly wishing that you could just let go of the guilt and the pain he caused you, so that you can let another man in.

You can, by simply telling yourself that your next man will not be like your last man.

When some of you date a new man, you start him off with a bank filled with 50 percent trust, or 25 percent trust. That man, every man, should start off at zero. I'm not saying that you can't trust him, but that he must earn your trust.

And let me tell you this. The favors you do for him, or the things you trust him with, should be consistent with the level of trust he's earned. And this is very important, so listen to what I'm saying here. If you give your man a short list to go to the grocery store with, and he brings back the three items on it, hurray! That means you can trust him to buy eggs, milk, and a loaf of bread. That doesn't necessarily mean you can trust him with your bank card and pin number to deposit the thousand dollars in cash you just gave him. Or just because you trust him with dropping your dog off at the vet when it was sick doesn't mean you should trust him to drop your fine girl-friend off at home one Saturday night when she's drunk.

This point should be clear. Unless you're willing to take the risk of getting burned, don't entrust that new man, or even your current man, with more responsibility than he's earned.

There's one more very important point I must make, because this seems to always get women in trouble. Ladies, men know you have big hearts. If you love us, we know there is nothing that you would not do for us, including opening up your purses.

Some men are so certain of this, they could be in a relationship that's not even a month old and will ask to borrow money from you. What should be a hard and fast rule is this—never lend money to the man you're dating or in a relationship with. Period.

I don't care how cute he is, or how he does the squiggle move that just lights all your candles—it doesn't matter. One way to walk away from a relationship without feeling as though you've been taken advantage of is to do it knowing that some man isn't holding on to twenty-five hundred dollars of your hard-earned money that you'll never see again.

That, along with feeling betrayed after trusting a man more than you should, is what will have you feeling as though you can't trust us anymore, which will ultimately lead you to believing you don't need us anymore.

If you trust a man only as much as you should, when the re-lationship ends you won't feel as though you've been victimized;

you'll feel only as though you're at the end of a relationship, which isn't all bad, because soon you'll be ready to start at the beginning of a new one.

Better all by yourself

I was speaking to my mother the other day on the phone. She told me how she married my father only a few months after her seventeenth birthday. She really didn't have any marketable skills. But, then again, women didn't need any in the fifties. A woman's intention then was to become a housewife.

My mother did that, but, like many women, after a while she became bored and wanted to work. My father owned a small real-estate business, and my mother asked if she could spend some time in the office and learn something that might one day allow her the opportunity to work.

My father said no, and was adamant about it. So my mother stopped asking.

My mother later found out that the reason for his denial was because there was a woman he employed that he was seeing.

Almost half a century later, my mother said to me, "If I was the woman that I am now, I wouldn't have cared what your father said. I would've marched right down there and learned what I needed to know to get a job."

As the old ad for Virginia Slims used to tout, "You've come

a long way, baby." And women have. I think it's a wonderful thing.

When you do the same work as men, you should be paid the same salary. You should be afforded all the opportunities we receive, and that is happening.

Hillary Clinton ran for president of the United States, and although she didn't win the nomination, she made history simply by being in the running.

You are in the workforce more now than you've ever been. You're attending college at a higher rate than men are, and you're buying your first homes at a younger age. That's a good thing, right? So why would you need us? You don't. That is, if your end goals in life are to buy a house, get a great job, then go to a sperm bank and make a purchase so you can have a kid or two.

If those are your plans, then yes, indeed, you can do better all by yourself.

But—and this may sound like antiquated thinking—if you want to find a partner, build a great friendship, fall in love, marry, have children, and raise them together, then maybe you might need a man after all.

Getting a man when you think you can do without

Okay, so you're thirty-one years old. If anyone would've asked you fifteen years ago where you would be now, you would've predicted that you'd be married and already had one baby, with another on the way. But you've been waiting, and you're still single, and what sense does it make?

You're tossing away money on rent when you could have bought a house three or four years ago.

So now is the time. You don't see any man coming along who's going to sweep you off your feet and take you house hunting, so you want to purchase one of your own.

Buy the house. That's a good move. More room, tax write-off, and all that stuff. And most good, successful guys love a woman with her own house. It displays a level of success and stability.

When it becomes a bad thing is when you list it as one of the reasons why men must be crazy not to be knocking down the door of that house just to get to you.

"I'm only thirty-one years old, and I got my own house. Most of those fools out there are still living with their mother," you tell your girlfriend.

And because you have that house, you start to strike from the list all the men who don't deserve a chance because they don't have a home of their own. But we've already discussed that in a previous chapter.

So, you're living in the big, new house, way out there in the suburbs, because they're nicer and cheaper out there. But when your cabinet door falls off, or your toilet backs up, you don't have the slightest idea of what to do.

Hmm, you think. Right now would be a good time to have that man around who I don't need.

What do you do? You'll think of something. It'll come to you.

But you're sleepy, so you think you'll turn out your bedside lamp and go to sleep. But half an hour later, after staring through the dark at the ceiling, you realize you can't go to sleep.

Why?

To be blunt, you're horny as hell, and there is nothing you can do about it.

But wait. You roll over, reach into your nightstand drawer, and pull out your trusty, battery-operated boyfriend. You give it a shot, but after fourteen consecutive nights with Mr. V, you find you're wanting something a little more "lifelike."

But no. You settle down, and you say the anthem to yourself over and over again—"I don't need a man!"—and fall into a restless sleep.

After another two months in your new home, your remotely operated garage door decides it prefers to be operated manually, there are three blown-out lightbulbs in your house that you could've changed weeks ago but you just don't feel like it, and you've been driving around on a little spare doughnut tire for the last nine days.

So you finally break down, telling yourself you don't need a man but sure would benefit from one just to fix things around the house. A fix-it guy.

You find one.

He's a hulking, muscular guy, not very attractive, has a missing tooth in the front of his mouth, and speaks with a lisp. But when he's performing the jobs you give him, he works in a wife-beater T-shirt, and his biceps are undeniable.

You end up in bed with him. He's the best lover you've ever

had. You have crazy moments, where for a split second you think you might be able to shape him into something presentable, something long-term, but you realize that would be like training your dog to wear pants and recite the ABCs.

You want to let DeeNatra (pronounced like Frank's last name, Sinatra) go, but you're whipped, wide open, and you can't get him out of your thoughts, even though you know he's sleeping with every girl he does home repairs for.

You find that you are angry, and bitter, and resentful, not of him but of yourself for putting yourself here. You told yourself you didn't need a man, didn't want one, so you believed you'd find your way around that, when all you had to do was change your thinking, then go out and get the man you really do want and maybe won't mind needing one day.

Most men believe that most women proclaim not to need a man for one simple reason: they can't get one. I don't believe that's true. I think there is someone for everyone. What I believe happened to the women who tell themselves they are better off without a man in their lives is that they've been hurt by a man who told them they loved them, said he would be there forever and would never leave them. Then one day he was gone. Poof!

Say this happened to you. After two years of being with the love of your life, you are alone, and to be quite honest, you no longer know how to deal. It just doesn't feel right not being in a relationship. So you hurry to jump into another one. You find a guy very similar to your last guy. Perfect, you think. You rush into a relationship, sleep with him, have him meet the family, tell him you love him, all the while secretly sizing him up for a wedding-day tuxedo. Then one day while you're telling him all about the trip you want to take with him a year from now, he turns to you and says that you're moving too fast, and he's done with you.

So, that puts you where? You had a long, committed relationship with a man you loved, which didn't work, and then you started another relationship with a man you were ready to give everything to, and that one didn't work, either. You tell yourself you've tried and tried, but no man wants you, so you come to the conclusion that you're better off by yourself. You'll be safer that way. You will no longer have love from a man, because no man wants you, but you won't risk the chance of your heart getting broken, and that's the most important thing.

But is it true that no man wants you? Absolutely not. Ladies, you might not want to hear this, but the truth is that the man you wanted, hell, all the men you've wanted who have left you, just didn't want you.

Now, I'm not trying to be critical. I'm not saying you're not good enough to be with the men that you chose in the past. What I'm saying is that you have to constantly check the levels of the man you're dealing with throughout the relationship to ensure that he's the man you should continue to devote your time, effort, and love to.

You should know this by now, but your man telling you he wants to be with you is not enough. When he turns to you and, between the spoonfuls of Cap'n Crunch he's shoveling into his mouth, says with little enthusiasm that he loves you should not be enough, either. He needs to prove it. You need to feel it, right?

You know when a man does more than just loves you, but is actively loving you. You know the difference, right?

When your man just loves you, he'll open the front door after you've been gone six hours without word, past the normal time you come home from work. He'll look worried, but when he sees you, he'll breathe a sigh of relief, tell you leftovers are in the fridge, then go back upstairs to bed.

A man who's actively loving you, upon opening that door, would grab you, hug you, kiss you, tell you how frightened he was. He would warm up your food, sit at the table with you, listen intently while you told him why you were late. Then he would lead you by the hand upstairs and make love to you, all the while kissing you, staring into your eyes, telling you not to ever scare him like that again.

What I'm saying is, the man you choose should want to be with you. He should prove it several times a day. Not consciously, as though he knows you're keeping a tally, but he should do things that prove he loves you just because.

A man like this will make you secure in your relationship, will not have you questioning yourself or your future with him. He will benefit from your love and your companionship. He will know that, and for that reason will want to do everything he can to thank you for that. He will therefore do the things we know you ladies want us to do, need us to do.

When your tire needs changing, or the garage door needs repairing, all you'll have to do is say it once, and next time you hit the remote, the garage door will roll up just like new to reveal your car with its new tire on it.

You will become accustomed to that kind of treatment from your man, and you'll tell your girlfriends, without any doubt or hesitation, "I need my man. I don't know what I'd do without him." Partially because it's true, partially because you love him so much that you know that by saying it, it's not a sign of weakness but a declaration of that love, and partially because knowing how he treats you, you know he's not even considering going anywhere.

So for those of you out there who have been hurt over and over and over again, don't just get out of the game and deny yourself the love you desire and deserve from a good man by telling yourself you don't need one.

And even if that may be the truth, if you at least want one, put yourself back out there, open yourself up to the idea again, but make sure he is a man who never stops proving to you that he wants you, and is not just satisfied that you want him. The latter is the man who will walk away leaving you feeling as though you've given your all and have nothing to show for it.

Mother and father

Women want children. We all know that. Maybe not all of you, but most of you, want children, been wanting them since you held your first plastic-eyed, rubber-headed baby doll.

Again, the old-school way was to get married, then have the

kids. There have been a few alterations made to that plan. Now a child is born, it seems, whenever a child gets good and ready to be born — marriage or not.

Of course, it's not that simple. There are a number of complicated factors that determine when this magical miracle takes place. But the one I'm going to talk about is that biological clock implanted in your . . . your . . . well, it's somewhere in a woman's body.

Anyway, whether it's nature or all the new science that is being discovered, women know when the optimum time to have a child is, when it's getting late, and when there are just ten seconds left on the clock before it explodes.

Ten seconds in human time is like five years, so when a woman reaches the age of around twenty-nine or thirty, the countdown is on. You start looking around, trying to convince your boyfriend of three weeks why you two should get married, or you start looking for serious relationships.

But if either of those attempts don't work, some women remind themselves that they don't need a man — even to get pregnant and have a baby.

So you now go out looking for eligible guys, not to start a relationship with, or to marry, but just to have sex with and get impregnated by. Or you might ask a successful male friend of yours if he would mind doing the honors. Or you might have sex with a guy and tell him there's no need for a condom because you're on the pill when, umm, you're not. (Not saying you'd do it, but there are some people who would. C'mon, you know it.)

It doesn't really matter how you get pregnant. I'm focusing more on the fact that today many women feel it's okay to do it knowing full well that there will not be a man around for the birth, and that there's a good chance a man might not be around to help raise that child.

Not to continue to beat up on the woman I took out for pizza and her little squirt of a son, but there were many nights, after ten P.M., when I would speak to her on the phone and hear her son in the background, raising havoc.

She'd cover the mouthpiece and scream in the direction of his room, "Go to bed!" But then I'd hear him say, "No! I ain't sleepy!" The bugger was four years old.

She would laugh it off and say, "Oh, sometimes he thinks he's my boyfriend or something. He just talks to me any way."

Another female friend told me she didn't want to have a child before she had a man she knew would stay because she always saw single women walking around with their sons, treating them like the child was her boyfriend or something, because she didn't have a man.

One day, while listening to *The Michael Baisden Show*, women were calling in, proclaiming how they did not need the aid of a man to help them raise their little boys. They were confident they could be both mother and father, and some of them went as far as to claim they could do a better job by themselves.

All jokes about the lightbulbs going unchanged aside, ladies, if there is one reason why you need to get up off that foolishness about you not needing a man, it's this one: Your son needs a man — his father, or a father figure.

This needs to be said twice. Your son needs his father, or a father figure.

I'm not saying that you can't do a wonderful job by yourself. I know it can be done. I know that firsthand, because I'm a product of that type of upbringing. But for the eight years that my father was in the home with me, I learned so much.

My mother taught me how to be a man based on what she thought she knew. My father did it based on what he *did* know.

Some boys are better off without their fathers. Some fathers are just bad men. There are bad people in this world. So if that's the case, then you grab your brother and tell him to be the best uncle he can be. Or you grab your male friend, or your boyfriend. Because, ladies, in this case, and arguably this could be the only one, but in this case, you *do* need a man.

We have to see you as a good ex before considering you as a wife

What do you do when you get angry with your boyfriend or your ex-boyfriend? Do you explode? Do you scream and holler and sail dishes at him like Frisbees, when all he did was forget to buy toilet tissue? We pay attention to that.

A male friend of mine has one of those girlfriends whom every man wishes never to bump into. He loves her a great deal, and has been with her for a little longer than five years.

He cares for her so much that he can't see life without her, but she is so much of a tyrant that he knows his life would be hell if he were to marry her, and that one day they would end up divorced.

This woman loves him a great deal as well. The man never cheated on her. But there were times when she'd ring his phone so many times when he was out with me and some of our friends, he would just stop answering it. She knew that the man was out with us, knew when he would be finished, because he told her all that, but she'd call anyway.

There were times when he'd arrive home and her car would be parked outside his place, with her in it, when they had no plans of seeing each other that night. Upon seeing him step out of his car alone, she'd climb out of her own and say that she missed him so much, she just had to come and see him. It was after midnight, and my friend was not so stupid not to know that this was her way of checking up on him.

There were times when they'd argue about one thing or another, and she'd fight with him with so much passion and so much hatred, it seemed she had no intentions of them reconciling. After one particularly bad argument, he had to keep his car in my garage. He had learned his lesson after his girlfriend slit his tires three times, dragged her key across one side of his car, from taillamp to headlight, and one time, at 1:45 A.M., he peeked out of the curtains for no reason during a late-night trip to the bathroom to find her walking up to his car, shaking a can of spray paint. He stopped her before she was able to graffiti the hood of his car. He should've kicked her to the curb after that, but he didn't.

They're still together, and they still love each other deeply, but she is always asking him, me, and the rest of our friends why he hasn't proposed to her yet.

They've been together forever. Neither of them ever gets carded anymore before ordering alcohol, if you know what I mean, but she just doesn't get it.

I wonder, can you answer this simple riddle for her?

And if you're starting to get what I'm saying, then you know the answer is that her man needs to see her as a good ex-wife before he considers proposing to her.

Believe it or not, men think like that.

Ladies, we don't want our marriage to fail, but it happens so much—more than 60 percent of marriages end in divorce—that it's almost an inevitability. Now it seems there are three things you can't avoid in life: death, taxes, and divorce.

Why do we care so much about what happens after we divorce a woman if by divorcing her we're getting rid of her? If children were a product of this marriage, you know just as well as we do that there really is no true divorce. It's more like a permanent separation. We still have to deal with you, still have to talk to you, and see you on occasion. And this will last for the rest of the child's life.

So think about it, if you're dating a man, and you're all up in his face about every little thing—if you nag him and insult him and check up on him like he's a child, then, when you're with your girls, you're slapping them fives, like, "Yeah, I got my man in check. I'm grooming him to be exactly the type of husband I need"—you're only fooling yourself.

To tell you the truth, if you're that trying as a girlfriend, your man probably hasn't even started thinking about what it would be like to deal with you as an ex-wife, because he hasn't even been able to imagine your insufferable behind as his wife.

But this even goes for those of you who are good women most of the time, and only lose your minds when you're really pissed off.

I dated a girl who was a great woman. She was caring, attentive, and supportive. Her downfall was that she was also jealous and insecure. Whenever I was around, whenever I was perfect—returning her phone calls moments after I received them, giving her no reason to even question or doubt me as being the perfect boyfriend—she was wonderful.

But if I let a day go by without talking to her, she would start ringing my phone incessantly. After the first bright, cheery phone message, they would take a continual turn downward.

They would start out, "Hey, just calling to say hi. Give me a call back, sweetie." But after the fifth or sixth unanswered call, the message would sound something like, "I know you're getting this messages, mot$&%^*ker. And I know you're out with some b#@*h. You better call me back!"

Sometimes, I would intentionally not answer her calls just to see how vile she could become.

Yeah, that's right. I was testing her. And yeah, I know, you think that was wrong. But isn't it better to find out who you're dealing with when you can still simply walk away rather than after you've been married and have kids?

But don't think it's just me. We all test you. We do it because we want to see what your threshold of tolerance is. Because the deal is, we aren't perfect, we know that, and we need for you to know it.

We are going to mess up. And I mean really mess up. Like bet-the-house-on-a-football-game mess up. Or leave-the-newborn-at-the-post-office mess up.

So we feel that if you're giving us hell now, if you're behaving like you have to make us pay for every wrong we commit, how do you believe we think you'll behave once we're married? Worse, once we're divorced?

We don't want to know. And most men won't want to risk it.

CHAPTER EIGHT

Are You Really the One?

Your best friend had a really wonderful boyfriend. They were together for eight years. You often wondered why she hadn't married him, only to find out that she thought she would. She had just been waiting on his proposal.

She mentioned several times that she wanted to get married, and often let him know it. But he had put her off, and made her feel that she would one day get her wish. Then, out of the blue, your friend came to you in tears, informing you that she and her boyfriend had broken up.

The reason, he explained, was because he knew that she always wanted marriage, but he discovered that he wasn't the marrying type. With that in mind, he felt he was doing her a favor to let her go, so that she could finally find what it was she always wanted. Then three months later, you and your girlfriend were shocked to hear that her ex-boyfriend was now engaged, and the happy new couple was due to wed in a week.

What the hell happened?

We want the total package, but you'll do

Ouch! Right. That's not to say that you aren't the total package. You just might not be the total package for your particular man.

If you don't know what the "total package" is, I'll attempt to define it.

What qualifies as the total package depends on what man you ask. Generally, it's the woman who has all the qualities *he's* looking for—physical, behavioral, educational, moral, and financial. It's the woman of his dreams. The woman who, when he was younger, he saw himself married to once he became older.

So he searched and dated, and dated and searched, and couldn't find her. But then one day he found you. You weren't exactly what he was looking for. You weren't perfect in every way, but you were cute, and you made him laugh, and you were self-sufficient, and the sex you gave him was more than just okay, it was downright acceptable. So he decided he'd enter into a relationship with you.

But he also made another decision.

Ladies, you won't like what you're about to hear, but it's true. On that day he met you and decided you'd do, he also told himself you'd never be the woman he'd marry.

Understand that about this, he was certain. There was no gray area, the jury was not out, and he did not tell himself that maybe if he grew to love you, there'd be a chance for you one day. No. Many men know *exactly* what they're going to do with you, the "bridge woman," if you will, the day they meet you.

Okay, so what the hell is a bridge woman? you ask.

That's the woman who carries him over, entertains him, occupies his time, pleases him sexually, until he finds the woman he really wants to be with, the woman he really wants to marry.

Many men refer to this as "just around the corner syndrome"—putting the woman he's with on hold because he believes the one he really wants is just around the corner. But because he does this doesn't necessarily mean he's just killing time. No. Absolutely not. If you're a good woman, which most likely you are, he's enjoying the relationship. And he's also taking advantage of a huge favor you're doing him.

What's the favor? you ask.

You're elevating his floor. And what I mean by that is, say you're college-educated, you have your own condo, you earn a better-than-average salary, and you always make sure he's satisfied in bed, even if sometimes he treats you like a blow-up doll. Considering the women he was dating before you—who had only finished high school, lived at home or with roommates, and were always asking for loans—your new man realizes he made a step up.

And being a smart man, he told himself he would not see another woman on the side unless she accomplished more than you, had a better body, gave him better sex, and was better educated.

So, getting back to the great relationship the two of you are having. Yes, he's enjoying himself, but there are some things he won't do with you, despite how wonderful that relationship may seem.

This is one of the ways you can tell if this is the man who will one day propose to you, or if he's just waiting for his total package.

You constantly suggest going on vacation together, but he always puts you off. The reason—he doesn't want to do the type of things with you that he's reserving for the woman he will marry. One, he doesn't want you getting misled, or at least more misled, by trips and memorable days spent in foreign countries. He doesn't want those photos taken that you'll frame and place on your mantel and stare at, telling yourself that one day he will be your husband.

More important, he doesn't want to spend the money, especially when he feels you're just a bridge woman, and the type of money that's spent on vacation is strictly for long-term, marriage material—total-package women.

Another sign that your man may not be around long is if he won't make major commitments. Say you want to move in together. "Why waste money living in separate houses?" you ask him.

Well, because maintaining his own place allows him to still search for the woman he really wants to be with. He doesn't really say that. He's just thinking it. But know that if it were you he wanted to be with, he would jump at the chance of having you pay half the cost of his mortgage or rent.

Another way of knowing you have no place in his future is because you're never mentioned. Some men will give you this clue without being aware that they're doing so.

He may be speaking about his plans for the future. He might mention moving to another city to pursue a new career. He might speak of starting a business, or making a drastic change in his life, but when you listen to how this will affect you, you hear nothing. That's because it won't affect you, other than the fact that he will no longer be in your life.

He hasn't included you in those future plans because he's not planning on being with you that long.

If your man won't meet your family or friends, or spend time with them around the holidays, it's because, believe it or not, he feels bad about deceiving you. He doesn't want to go fooling your folks, uncles and aunts, have them thinking he might one day marry you, when he knows there's nothing further from the truth.

He knows it's best to keep his distance, keep things between just the two of you, so when he does leave, he'll save you the embarrassment of all your people asking, "Whatever happened to John Boy? We really liked him."

And last, do you ever feel that your man is hiding something? No, not a dead body in the closet, but maybe his emotions. Ever feel as though he's not opening up to you like you think he should, or is capable of? Maybe every time you give him a passionate kiss and tell him you love him, he taps you on the chin with his fist and replies, "You know, you're not so bad yourself."

Or maybe it's not that straightforward. Maybe there's just a feeling you get after sex, that sinking notion that he's not as devoted to your relationship as you are.

If you feel that, it's probably because it's true.

He's keeping that distance because he doesn't want to fall so deep that when he finally finds his total-package woman, he'll have problems leaving you. So he builds that wall, hides his feelings, but still gives you enough to keep you present until he's ready to move on.

But if all else fails . . .

Yes, a lot of men might use you as a rest stop on their journey to finding that perfect women. But for one reason or another, some men never locate *her*—the one.

Those men may find themselves tired, or just unwilling to go any further. And what I mean by this is that maybe your man has overestimated himself and his value to the type of woman he's hoping to replace you with. Maybe during the course of your six-or eight-year relationship, every time he approached one of those total packages, they looked him up and down, replayed in their heads the lame line he had spoken to them, then covered their mouths and tried not to laugh as they hurried away.

After too much of that, a man either gets tired or gets the point.

Like I said, you're a good catch in your own right, or he wouldn't have stayed with you as long as he has. And he has developed feelings for you. Yes, he was hiding many of those feelings, preparing for the day when he would drive off into the sunset with his beautiful new bride, but now he's realized you're the best thing he might ever get, especially considering he's had zero success with everyone else.

I get the feeling that you're not liking what I'm saying here, but you *have* been with him all those years, and you *have* been wanting him to marry you for, like, half of those years. And most likely, if I didn't tell you that he was going to propose to you only because no one else was interested, you would have never known.

As I said before, he does love you, or he couldn't have stayed with you as long as he has, so what difference does it make?

For other men entertaining marrying their bridge woman, it's not that they cannot interest a woman they consider perfect. It's that after all those years with you, he finally stumbles upon the realization that you are exactly the woman he has been looking for.

You'll know this is the case with your situation if you've been dating the same guy for several years—the guy who always dodges the subject of marriage when you bring it up. He never gives you any concrete reasons other than that he's just not ready. Then one day—the next holiday, or your relationship anniversary, or even just Saturday at dinner—he'll surprise you with a ring, and ask for your hand.

When this happens, most likely it's because your man took a hard look at his situation. He may have been lying in bed, realizing he is on the verge of thirty-nine or forty-one years old. He doesn't have a child yet, when he always thought he would have had at least three by this age. He considers his best friends, who are all more than forty years old, still hanging out at clubs, still using those same one-liners they used ten years ago, and still getting blown off as harshly.

Then your man will think about you, the steadfast partner you've always been, all the good qualities you have, and how you've loved him for the past twelve years. That's when he'll ask himself, why had he been waiting, when the woman he is supposed to marry was right in front of him?

You're the lucky one

Don't look at this as if you're what's behind door number two. Hey, you're the one he proposed to, the one he's going to marry, and if it helps, the competition was much stiffer than you probably realize.

What I'm saying is that the total-package woman I mentioned

lives largely in your man's dreams. Realistically, how many total-package women are there out there? A woman who is supermodel beautiful, with the body of an Olympic gymnast, the sexual skill of a highly paid prostitute, the salary of a brain surgeon, and the desire to cook, clean, and raise children like a fifties housewife? That's what your man considers perfection, and that woman is not standing on every street corner, waiting on a bus.

So that was your competition. No wonder you won, right? But unfortunately there were others.

You don't want to hear this, but up until the point when a man is certain that it's you he's going to propose to, most men still maintain relationships with two or three other women. He probably wouldn't have been seeing them as long as you, but the level of his relationships with them would have been nearly as deep or possibly even more meaningful than yours.

These women are the ones he picked up along the way, thinking, hoping, that one would be the perfect woman, but later, upon getting to know them, he realized they couldn't even come close to you. But they were good enough, as you were, to continue seeing. So he did.

But since taking account of his life, and understanding that it was best for him to claim one of you and settle down, he knew he had to lighten his load.

The number of men I know who have had to make lists to determine which one of the three or four women they were seeing would be the lucky one they finally decide to marry is almost unbelievable.

I know, it's just terrible. But he chose you. Why? Because he loves you the most, or because you make the most money, or because you were the best-looking, or gave him the best sex, or might have the prettiest babies, or nags him the least, or any number of reasons why a man chooses to marry a woman.

You're asking, "Do some men really choose a wife by some of the qualities you just listed?"

Sure, they do.

Women do the same thing. You'll marry a man because he makes an obscene amount of money, or you'll convince yourself that you love him because that thing he does when you're in bed can only be love, right?

But despite the way he came to his conclusion, he picked you. And one thing you can feel good about is, if he went through the trouble of dumping the other women he shared relationships with, that generally means that he wants to carry none of them into his marriage. You're the woman he chose, so you're the woman he wants to be committed to.

Now, if you've been dating the same guy for several years and he has not proposed, or you just met the man of your dreams and you'd love to see yourselves arm in arm, strolling down that rose-petal-covered aisle sometime in the near future, let me offer you a little advice.

CHAPTER NINE

Ten Steps to Make Him Ask,
"Will You Marry Me?"

Now that you know many of the reasons why men fear marriage, and some things you might be doing wrong that might prevent you from marrying, you'll want to know what you can do to increase your chances of one day receiving that proposal.

I can help with that.

The list I'm about to present to you, believe it or not, will work equally as well for women who have been in a relationship for only six months as it will for those of you who have been dating a man for several years, and even for those women who have yet to find the man they want to marry.

Yes, there will be tailoring you must do in order for the steps to fit your individual needs, and, as with everything worth having, hard work is required, as well as your brains and your female intuition. But if you initiate the steps in this plan, the man you have carefully chosen should fall madly in love with you, recognize the insurmountable value you add to his life, and then, if he has even half the sense of a three-year-old, he will propose to you.

If he does not, trust that it is due to no fault of your own, and honestly recognize that he is a man you are better off without.

1. Find the right man, and be sure that he wants marriage

Ladies, let me stress this point. This is the most important step of the ten. If you don't perform this step correctly, then the remaining nine will prove worthless. So many of you wonder why after dating, falling in love, and having relationships with so many men, you haven't been asked to marry one of them.

The answer is really very simple. None of those men wanted marriage, at least not at the time they dated you.

Sadly, many women believe relationships still work the way they did in our parents' and grandparents' generations when a young man searched for a young woman with the sole intention of marrying her. They dated to get to know each other, and they got to know each other hoping to fall in love, which in turn gave them reason to marry. In our parents' and grandparents' day, this was what the man wanted from the start, so he pushed for it until he received it.

Today things are different, and many of you have yet to realize that. Today, a man searches for companionship and sex. His goal is to have someone to go to the movies with, and someone to aid him in releasing his stress when he's horny. So he finds that woman and dates her and takes her to the movies, which allows him to get to know her, and getting to know her will, he hopes, ultimately allow him to have sex with her. That's it. Mission accomplished.

I mean, what more do you expect from your eighteen-year-old boyfriend, or your twenty-three-, or twenty-seven-or even thirty-three-year-old boyfriend? That, after all those great movie dates and all that great sex, he'll say, "You know what? I want to have great movie dates and great sex with you for the rest of my life. Let's get married!"

No. It doesn't work that way. A man doesn't marry you because you want him to, or because you wish he would. A man marries you because he wants to marry. He's not looking for you, he's looking for a wife. He met you, and he decided that you were perfect. So, he marries you. But if a man is not looking for marriage, no matter what you do, he will not propose.

"But what if he falls in love?" you ask.

Love has nothing to do with it. If men married every woman they fell in love with, most men would've been married since they were twenty-one years old, and probably have six wives a piece. Men do love the women they marry, but they don't marry just because they're in love. Men marry because they want to raise a family. Men marry because they want to combine incomes. Men marry because they are tired of buying drinks, and spitting game, and waiting for your phone calls. Men marry because it's time. And men marry because they don't want to have to beg and plead for sex every time they want satisfaction.

In our grandparents' generation, most men courted women— would take her out to dinner, to a show, bought her flowers, hoping she would find him suitable enough to marry. What those men really wished for was sex, but knew they'd never get it before rings and vows were exchanged, because they knew their girlfriends' shotgun-toting fathers would have none of that.

The point I'm making is that when your grandfather saw your grandmother and decided he would start courting her, he didn't love her at that point. He couldn't have. He had seen her in the schoolhouse only three times.

Your grandfather, like men today, decided he would marry because he had a need to fulfill—a specific need.

Understand this. If back then young men were getting as

much sex as they get today, without ever thinking about marrying a woman, do you really think as many of our grandfathers would have married our grandmothers?

So, what you really need to understand, if you want marriage, is that you should be dating a man who *wants* marriage as well, and knows he wants it.

2. Inform him of your plans for marriage, including the date

As I've said, things are different now. Just because you're dating a guy who loves you and you love him doesn't mean he'll one day want to marry you. When conducting your search, or when hanging out, or when allowing a man to say hello to you on the street, when you decide to take it to that next level—if you're looking for marriage—you have to make sure that's where his head is at, too.

And just how do you go about doing that? Open your mouth and ask.

That's right, and you don't even have to be subtle about it, although it wouldn't hurt.

The deal is, if you're with a man who finds you attractive, thinks you're a good catch, and is actually looking for marriage, when you ask him about it, he'll jump at the chance to tell you what a great institution he believes marriage to be. He's going to want to impress you.

For the guy who isn't interested in that, depending on how blatant you are ("I want a man to marry me. Are you that man?"), he might choke on his Merlot, or excuse himself to use the men's room, then climb out the window, never to return. But that's fine with you, right? One less man you have to worry about spending several years with.

So, of all the men who have been approaching you, or whom you've mustered the courage to approach, you've chosen the one you liked most. You first met for coffee, and on the next date you met at a restaurant and had a wonderful dinner, which you so gratefully paid for. And during that meal you weren't pushy or desperate, but you made your case. You let that man know that you were dating not just to date, or to ultimately have sex, but to find a good man, a man you would want to spend the rest of your life with. And because you're now (fill in the age) and not getting any younger, you could see yourself married in (fill in the blank) years.

That is the tricky part. Most men, and definitely the men who are in no way thinking about marriage, will be put off. You'll know by the bead of sweat that races down the side of his face, and the way his eyes start darting back and forth in search of the nearest exit.

But the man who wants what you want, the right man, will appreciate you telling him this, and respect you for it. You're giving him a heads-up, letting him know that you're not a woman who is just out to sleep around, and at the very least it's giving him an out. And if he is a good and respectful man, he'll tell you, either down the road as that date approaches or even over that dinner, "I'm sorry, but I'm not looking for marriage right now." Or, "I'm not looking for marriage that soon, so I'm probably not the man for you. But maybe we can still be friends."

But for the sake of our list, let's assume he is the guy you were hoping he'd be, and he says something like, "I perfectly understand. I'm [fill in the age] years old myself, and I've always wanted to marry. I'm just waiting for the right woman to tell me she can tolerate me." (Cute, self-deprecating humor. Isn't he wonderful!)

3. Make regular dates with him, inside and outside the house

You've had three dates with your chosen guy, and he seems like he might be the real deal. You realize that you share similar likes and dislikes, and his head is where yours is regarding the whole marriage thing. He doesn't seem like the type, at least at this point, who will jump out of bed, abandon you, leaving his underwear on the carpet, moments after you tell him you love him.

So, if he indeed is the guy you want in your future, how do you make that happen?

Well, obviously, you have to continue to see him on a regular basis. Dates should be made at least two or three days of the week. And don't worry, you won't be forcing things. What's two days out of seven, especially when the only thing both of you are probably doing on those other five days is coming home from work, watching TV, and going to bed by yourselves.

You make plans to see him, let's say on a Monday, and then, before ending the date, you ask when you'll see him again, or suggest that you hang out on Thursday. Most likely you won't even have to do that. If he likes you the way you like him, he'll be the one asking for future dates, because, remember, he's in this to win you.

Something you should know, ladies, is that when a man finds a good woman, one he believes will make him a good wife, he'll want to wrap her up and take her off the market as soon as possible. He knows other men are looking for the same thing, so he'll want to snatch you up before someone else has the opportunity to spark your interest.

Again, the dates should be a regular thing, and time should be equally spent inside the home, your place or his, as well as out. You don't want to get in the rut of having him come over, bringing a DVD, and you guys sharing a bottle of wine, which will lead to fooling around, then him taking your hand and leading you to your bedroom.

Of course, there will be times when those moments will be shared. Remember, we aren't living in our grandparents' time, and most women want to see what their chosen man is working with before they buy the goods, just like men want to see what their chosen woman has to offer.

The important thing is not to indulge in that too soon.

I've always been of the belief, at least when dating just to date, that it doesn't matter when the first sexual encounter is had. If two consenting adults meet, want sex from each other that first night, and agree to have it, the man shouldn't and many times won't consider the woman fast, or a slut, because she engaged.

But when you're dating a man you have chosen as your potential husband, you have to make that guy wait. Not an unreasonable amount of time—not a year—just a respectable amount, maybe a month or two, tops. Don't worry, he won't walk away. If he selected you because he sees you in his future, he understands that the two of you could potentially be together for the rest of your lives. What's the hurry?

So date as much as the two of you want to. I say at least two, but you may see him as many as five, times a week early on. What this does is fast-track the dating/getting-to-know-you process. It gets you to that comfortable place quicker, where you're sharing your pop-corn in the movie theater, where he's eating from your plate, and where you both start to feel that your time together really could be the start of something much bigger.

4. Communicate frequently, via phone, text, or e-mail— create a pattern

What man, or woman, for that matter, doesn't like regularity and consistency? When you were a child, if your mother came into your room and kissed you good night each night before you fell asleep, you appreciated that for two reasons. One, because the act told you she cared, and two, because you cared for her, and knowing you would see her gave you something to look forward to.

Constant communication in a relationship works the same way, but it does a couple of other things as well. Let's say your chosen guy works in an office. He's having a busy morning; maybe something hasn't gone just the way he wanted it to. His phone rings. It's you. Your voice is cheery and chipper. Upon hearing it, either he'll immediately perk up or he'll let you know that he's having a rough morning. Either way, you're helping him out, and bringing him just a little bit of joy. If his mood doesn't improve because he's initially happy to hear you, you, being the great woman you are, will say something funny, or make a naughty comment about what the two of you did last night, which will bring him out of his funk. Trust me, he'll appreciate that.

But don't stop there. You want your communication with him to be consistent. And I'm not speaking of nagging, or calling him and talking on the phone for hours like you did when you were thirteen. There should be a reason for your calls. The reasons don't have to be serious. You could call him back at one-thirty that afternoon just to ask him if his day has improved. He'll say yes, and you'll say, "Great! If you told me those people were still messing with you, I was gonna come over there." Then you say good-bye.

You want to keep those calls short and sweet, because he's busy, and you are, too.

If you call him at ten in the morning because you know at this time things aren't really busy yet, then call him every couple of days at that time. This will brighten his day, and eventually he'll get used to hearing from you, just like he had gotten used to that kiss from his mother before bed. And I guarantee you, if for some reason you aren't able to call, you'll find him ringing your phone at ten in the morning. It will have become a ritual, and this is good for you.

Now not only is he thinking about you when you're at his place or the two of you are out together, but he's thinking about you at 9:58 A.M., anticipating your phone call.

But there's more. That text function on your cell phone—is that not the greatest little invention or what? This is another way that you can let him know you're thinking about him, and vice versa. Sometimes the texts you send don't have to be returned. You don't even send them expecting a response.

"I HOPE MY LAST CLIENT GETS STUCK IN THE ELEVATOR FOR THE REST OF THE DAY!!!"

There really isn't a response to that, but you're letting your guy in on some of the nonsense you may have encountered during the day. It lets him know that you're thinking about him, and that he's not the only one dealing with knuckleheads all day.

E-mail works, too. But it's not as effective as phone or text, or as immediate. But if that's the only way you can access him, then use it.

A quick word on the communication thing, though I don't know why I feel the need to tell you this, ladies, because it's always you who keep telling us that we don't communicate enough. Anyway, making a date on Monday to see your guy on Thursday and then not speaking to him over that period of time just won't work.

I hate to say it, but I stopped dating a woman because I had too much of a hard time getting hold of her. I would call her cell and leave cheery messages, or send her "JUST THINKING ABOUT YOU" texts, only for her to reply to them hours later, if at all. That led me to believe, at best, that she was too busy to think about me, and at worst, she just plain *wasn't* thinking about me.

And no, this type of communication is not mandatory in order to land your guy, but it goes a long way in the effort toward doing so. Trust me.

One more thing: if your guy does not return your texts or your e-mails, or seems bothered every time he picks up the phone, he might feel as though you're nagging him. If you call or text only every now and then, you aren't nagging him; he just doesn't want to hear from you that often. And I don't have to tell you that if that's the case, he won't want to deal with you for the next twenty, thirty, or maybe fifty years of your life. Take this as a hint, a gift, even, and bail out before you get emotionally attached and find yourself accepting his unwillingness to communicate with you.

5. Choose two nights of the week to have dinner together

Let's say a Monday and a Wednesday, or a Tuesday and a Thursday, but keep them the same, so that both you and he can plan around those days. You want you and your guy to get closer, but you also want him to continue to spend time doing the things he was doing before he met you, whether playing pool with the guys, watching football games, or taking those evening graduate courses.

Do you see what we're doing here with this step? A few things. The first is, we're staying consistent. Just like the kiss from his mother and the phone calls from you at ten in the morning, your guy will look forward to seeing you on Tuesday and Thursday nights. If on Tuesday he's having a rough day at work, he'll be able to shrug that off easier than if it were Monday, because he knows he's going to see you later.

The second is, he knows he's going to get a home-cooked meal. What man would not take pleasure in that? If you still don't believe the huge importance men place on a good meal, ladies, please, put this book down for a moment and call your grandmothers and let them school you on that.

The third is that you're giving him another example of how much you like him, how much you care. Men take note of that. Wrongly, we might not always say "thank you," or tell you how delicious the food was, but believe me, we notice what you're doing.

And the fourth, and probably the most important, thing that these biweekly dinners on the same two nights of the week are doing is giving him some insight into what Tuesdays and Thursdays might be like with you if the two of you were to ever marry.

This is key. So very, very important.

It's like that five-year-old kid you always see in commercials, standing on the edge of the swimming pool with the inflatable arm floats around his little biceps. His dad is in the water, doing everything in his power to try to coax him in, but the kid isn't budging.

That's us—that's men. We aren't jumping into marriage, because it's big, and vast, and deep, and scary, and we know guys who have drowned in that mess.

But that father is smart. He splashes around in the water, slaps some up at the kid. The kid feels the water hit him in the face, and it's not that bad. It's actually kind of warm, and Dad does look like he's having a good time in there.

So that's what dinner is—the feel of that warm water.

It's the first step of many that will let your guy know that marriage with you just might not be that bad after all. If nothing else, after just two weeks of four great meals, and great conversation, and candles, and wine, he'll tell himself that was far better than four nights of peanuts, Oreo cookies, and Gatorade.

So maybe, after who knows how many more dinners and the other efforts you're putting forth, he'll eventually dive into that pool of marriage, and find out the water is just fine.

6. Enjoy what he enjoys, and introduce him to what you love

What is the most flattering thing you can say to describe your guy? How about, "He's my best friend." That's a good one, right? I've heard many women say that's what they want of their man. Believe it or not, we want the exact same thing.

But we may voice it a little differently.

When a man is lucky enough to find a woman who shares an interest and participates in what he likes, he might say, "She's cool, because she's just like a dude. She's like one of my boys, but she's a chick."

This might not sound flattering to you, but it's almost the highest compliment a woman can receive from her man.

So how do you attain that high level of being "just like a dude"?

You have to do what your guy does, enjoy what he enjoys. And don't worry about invading his personal time. He wants you to participate in his pastimes, because he knows that it will bring the two of you closer.

So when a guy asks you, "Hey, do you like football?" and you turn your nose up and purse your lips like a mosquito just flew into your mouth, you're rejecting the perfect opportunity to gain access into his life. If you aren't a fan, what you might want to say is, "Sure, I like it, but I don't know the rules."

What he'll say is, "No problem. I'll teach you." And you both win, because we love feeling that we're teaching our woman something she doesn't already know, and you win because football is really a cool game, and once you do learn the rules you're going to love it as much as we do. I promise.

So let me tell you what happens after that. You'll be invited to all the Monday night football games he watches, either at his place, his friends' places, or bars. And a byproduct of that is that you'll get to meet all his friends—something else that you really want. But we'll get to that in the next step.

So, you start watching football, and that adds to the time you spend together with your man. Who knows, maybe you'll give Xbox360 or PS3 a try. I know, you're saying, "Don't get carried away." But you'll reap the same benefits. You really will.

Now, I know what you're about to say. You shouldn't be the only one who has to open up and embrace new things, right? You're absolutely right.

One of the wonderful things about dating someone is that that person is different, with different beliefs, different experiences, and different likes.

So if you like biking, then get him into that. Not only will you have more time together, but you'll both be working at staying fit.

Or if you like live music and he's never been into that, he will appreciate you opening up that form of entertainment to him.

The deal is, you'll both grow, you'll both gain, and he'll know that if he hadn't met you, he would have never been introduced to all the fun and wonderful things you two now participate in. Which gives good argument to why he should consider being with you for the rest of his life, huh?

7. Meet his friends, and his mother—let your guy know how others see you

"Why haven't I met any of your friends or family?" you asked your old boyfriend.

Whatever reason he gave was a lie if he didn't say, "Because we aren't that serious. I'm not planning on being with you for very long. So why have them meet you and like you on Thanksgiving, when you might very well be gone by Christmas?"

But you asked that question because you knew his friends and family were important to him. You knew that if you could just impress them, they might argue for you, convince your guy that he should choose you. And you were absolutely right.

So, obviously, if you have an opportunity to meet that circle of people who know your man the best, then you should take it. Even if that means learning the rules of football.

Okay, so you did what you were supposed to do in step 1, because I told you how important that was, and that all the other steps would be useless if you weren't successful with that one. But because you were successful, your chosen guy is asking you to hang out with him and his friends.

Understand that this is a huge deal. He wants to bring you along, not because there's a two-person minimum when visiting his friend's place but because he's proud to have you by his side, and he wants to show you off.

But it might not be just that. If he is considering you, like you are him, then maybe he has a little something up his sleeve, and wants to get his friend's opinion of you.

When this chance arises, regardless of who you're meeting, you should always put your best foot forward. Be yourself, of course. No need to try to impress, because your guy already believes you're impressive. Just be your everyday, adorable, sociable, intelligent, humorous, perfect self. No pressure, right?

So you two hang out, and naturally you're wonderful, and all his friends think so. But they don't say anything then, so that you won't be aware of their thoughts. His male friends will only really give you a hard look when your back is turned, so they can see how your jeans fit, or when his back is turned, so he won't see them checking out how your jeans fit.

And the girlfriends of his friends will bat their eyes and give you plastic smiles until they really figure out what you're after. But if you're the good woman your guy hopes you are, those girls will warm to you.

So how does this work to your advantage?

Well, after he drops you off at home, your guy will call one of his friends and say, "Well, what do you think?"

Or, even more impressive, if you really made your mark, your guy's phone would have been vibrating in his pocket the entire drive back to your house from the calls of his friends, dying to tell him how great you are.

And yes, if for some reason he hasn't realized this, his friends will be quite honest and say, "You'd be as dumb as we always thought you were if you were to lose her. You'll never luck up like that again."

And of course, the same goes for his mother.

Meeting the friends is one thing. And although it's a big deal, a huge step, meeting the mother is like meeting the Pope, the president, and the Wizard of Oz, all rolled into one.

I would have to say that the most important reason, dare I say the sole reason, a man takes a woman for that initial meeting with his mother is to inform her that this might be the woman she will be calling "daughter in-law," and to ask his mother if he's making the biggest mistake of his life.

If she likes you, she'll tell him he's making the right decision. And if she loves you, and has always wanted her son to marry, she'll even campaign for you. Wouldn't that be great!

Obviously, if she thinks you're horrible—a money-grubbing, back-stabbing woman, who, once married, will do nothing but rest on the sofa, pop out babies, and watch judge shows all day—she'll tell him that, as well.

So make a good impression. And yes, you can put forth a little extra effort in this situation.

8. Acquire space in his place, then spend some nights

Okay, so that earring you said you accidentally left in the cushions of your guy's sofa—we know that's a plant you expect another woman to find. Or how about the panties you left without, as well as your hair clip. Guys search for those things not long after you leave, to make sure there are no land mines planted that will explode the minute another woman uncovers them. So stop "accidentally" leaving them. We're onto you.

Now, the bath gel in the shower, along with your purple scrunchie hanging from the showerhead, that's a little different. Some of you are so bold that you don't even ask permission to leave your things behind. You just pull off your shower cap and hang it on the hook till your next shower, kind of marking your territory.

That works for the women who are bold enough to do it. I mean, what are we supposed to do? We just had sex with you, yelled out your name, proclaimed how great you are, then what? We tell you we don't want your stinkin' honey-maple-cucumber bath gel in our shower?

In my experience, there really is no "best" way for you to acquire space in your guy's place. There are ways that work better than others, though. As I just noted, the bathroom is a good place to start. It's just common sense. If you're spending time over there, taking showers, then you'll want your own things. Unless you prefer how your guy's no-name deodorant soap from the dollar store makes your skin feel.

He should understand it's simply all about need, supply, and acceptance.

If he likes you to spend a good amount of time at his place, there are some things you're going to need, such as a toothbrush. And if he doesn't supply those things, then he should accept you supplying your own.

The same goes for loungewear. Say you don't want to scuff up his hardwood floors with your high heels, and don't like walking barefoot. You'll want fuzzy socks to wear, or slippers. You might want to mention that fact, and if within a week or two he hasn't bought you a pair, which would most likely be the case, then bring your own and leave them.

That also goes for nightgowns and lingerie; that is, after you get tired of walking around in his big T-shirts. It also goes for extra pairs of undergarments, and maybe even a shirt or two, just in case you have a wardrobe malfunction and you need to make a change.

There are a few reasons you want to do this. The first is the reason you've been giving him: convenience. You can brush your teeth at night, bathe using what you're accustomed to, and sleep in clothes that don't have the sleeves hacked off.

The second reason is that you want your guy to get accustomed to sharing his space with you. You want him to trip over your stuff, have to move aside your body butter or foot scrub when reaching for his shaving cream. If nothing else, that will keep you on his mind even when you're not around.

The third reason is the most underhanded. Your things will advertise to another woman (that is, if there is another woman) that your guy is already seriously involved.

And don't feel overconfident that your guy isn't seeing someone else just because you left your nail polish and your hairbrush at his place. When we're expecting other company, we have no problem hiding those few items; then, in preparation for your next visit, we'll simple return them to their exact places.

But if you leave undergarments, shoes, toiletries, a jacket, a couple of fashion magazines on the coffee table, most guys would consider it easier just to stay faithful to you rather than try to shift all your stuff to a closet, then have to wrack our brains trying to remember the exact place where each item should be returned.

And if nothing else, this will update you as to whether he still feels the same way about the destination of your relationship.

If your guy has no problem with you washing your panties in the shower, then hanging them out on the towel rack to dry, you know it's just you and him. If every time you come by, your toothbrush lands in a different place and your slippers are tucked deep in the closet instead of at the foot of the bed where you left them, then you know that you should probably rethink this guy.

9. Stay until morning, then go straight to work

I know, some of you are asking, What if I have little ones at home? You can still participate in these steps. Choose one night during the week, or wait till the weekend and arrange for your children's father, grandmother or your close friend to take the kids. You would do it for a vacation or business trip. This might be just as important. This might be the man you spend the rest of your life with. So, if you have kids or not, and if things move the way they naturally should, the way you both want them to, you'll find yourself spending some nights at his place. You'll want to be available for this to happen. This is about much more than simply not wanting to climb out of his bed, or him out of yours, right after sex and drive home in the middle of the night.

Spending the night together allows much more time to be spent doing something other than having sex. Namely, sleeping.

How the woman in our life sleeps with us is very important.

A friend told me he once dated a girl he was crazy about, but knew that he ultimately could not marry her because she snored like a stalling chainsaw. Some men — well, I shouldn't exaggerate — most men don't like women sleeping all up under them — her legs and arms entangled in his, her head upon his shoulder while he's trying to get some shut-eye.

We understand how women like that, so we'll participate for fifteen minutes, or until you fall asleep, whichever comes first, then we scramble away, get our distance, spread out, so we can knock out.

Do you hog the blankets? Do you talk incessantly while your guy is trying to fall asleep? All these things we learn about you by having you spend the night. And while you're there, other things will happen as well.

There will be pillow talk.

There seems to be no conversation more open, honest, and stress-free than conversation had after sex. This is a great time to gauge where your guy is in your relationship, because he's not pulling punches. He's just been given what he wanted most, or at least wanted most at that moment, and has no reason to tell falsehoods or mislead you. Ask a guy before sex, while you're dangling the act over his nose like a carrot and half of them will tell you he'll marry you if you just give him what he's begging for.

But that's not the only way to get an idea of how much he might be feeling for you.

Yeah, he pushes you away while he's trying to fall asleep, but during the night, if he really cares for you, you might wake up briefly to feel him wrapped around you, or when the alarm clock goes off in the morning, you might find yourself in a hug that he initiated.

If you're nothing more than a piece of tail that he sleeps with and allows to stay over, there will most likely be no affectionate contact during the night.

But you know that's not the case with you. So, you stay over a couple of nights a week, and get up extra early to race home, shower, get dressed, and head back in the direction you just came to go to work.

For all the obvious reasons, you should tell your guy that maybe it would be best when you spend the night that you start leaving for work from his place. You'll tell him it will give you more time to sleep in, you won't have to drive as far, and you can avoid a lot more traffic.

In your mind you know you'll eventually bring a few work outfits over, giving you a bit more space in his closet. But not only that, the two of you will wake, shower, and get dressed in the morning together. And isn't that what people do when they're married?

See, that is what often stops men from pulling the marriage trigger—they fear what will happen after the gun goes off. But like

I said before, if you give men what they sincerely think will be an accurate simulation of marriage, they might tell themselves that it's not that bad at all, and soon they won't be able to live without you. That's exactly what you want to happen.

So now that you're waking, showering, and dressing in the morning together, there's one more thing that should happen.

You've got to eat together.

The key is for the two of you to sit down after you've showered and dressed and start the day together, and have a little more conversation.

Now, imagine, that's in addition to the conversation you had last night, after the great sex you gave him. Then, while at work, he's going to call you, you'll text him, he'll think about some of the things you two spoke about this morning, which means he probably won't go a full twenty minutes without having at least one thought about you. Wouldn't that be great?

10. Integrate yourself in his day-to-day—become irreplaceable

We all know that everyone needs someone. What you should also know is that your guy needs and wants you. If that weren't true, he wouldn't still be around after the three months, or the year, or the fifteen months, that you guys have been getting to know each other.

The reason why he comes to your house and eats the meals

you cook for him, or the reason why he introduced to you his mother, is because he is really serious about you, and he just might be on the verge of deciding that it's you he wants to ask to be his wife.

Trust me, he's scared to death. He's shaking in his tube socks. He probably even stares wide-eyed at you while you're sleeping at night, asking himself if he's really serious about doing this. But believe me, despite the fear, he's at least thinking about it.

So you ask, if he's at least thinking about it, how do you make him certain about it?

This is the easiest step of the ten, and requires that you do nothing more than what you've already been doing. Spend time with your guy—run errands with him, sit on the sofa and watch TV together, have sex, paint the bathroom, clean the closet, and rake the leaves. Do all the stuff that happens in the average relationship, everything that happens in the average marriage.

And as I mentioned before, what scares men is not knowing what marriage will be like. If you can give him that glimpse, if you can present a fairly accurate representation, one that he enjoys, one that he knows he can live the rest of his life in, I guarantee you, he will start pricing rings.

By doing that with your guy, he will become more and more comfortable with you. Remember consistency? If every time he watches his favorite show you're there beside him, waiting to give him spirited conversation afterward, he'll get used to that. If he always hated shopping for groceries, but with you it's much more tolerable, or even fun, he'll appreciate you for that, and possibly never want to go grocery shopping without you again. Hmm, what will he have to do to make that a reality? Say it with me . . . wedding ring.

But there is a lot more going on here than just being around when he wants help doing laundry. Integrating yourself in his life means that he is opening up his life to you, and if he does that, that means he trusts you. And that's one of the biggest battles a woman will have to win in order for a man to surrender himself to her.

A gentleman I interviewed told me that he had been dating a woman for two months. He was interested in marriage, but he didn't know if she was the one. They were having a good time together. He spent a lot of time at her place hanging out, when one day, he received a phone call informing him that his mother had been involved in a serious accident.

"I told her I had to go," the gentleman told me. "I told her what happened and told her I'd call her when I found out more. She told me she wanted to go with me. I told her no, but she insisted, telling me that she wanted to be there for me."

He said that the accident was more serious than he had thought. His mother was in intensive care for three weeks, and teetered on the verge of losing her life several times. He spent many nights there at her bedside until she was released. Each and every time, his girlfriend was there with him. Often, she even came and sat with his mother when he was at work.

"She didn't have to do that," he said. "I mean, I knew her for only two months, but she stuck with me during what I think was the toughest time in my life. If that didn't let me know that this was the woman I wanted by my side forever, I don't know what would."

Needless to say, he told me they married nine months later.

The reason why? At least part of it, I'm sure, was because that woman became irreplaceable to him just by being by his side and caring about what he cared about. Although we wish similar events on no one, occurrences like that bring couples together. But that's not to say they have to be tragic, near-death experiences. If your guy has had a hard day at work and you're there to comfort him, or if he's failed an exam, botched an interview, or lost his job, you being there to support him, help him out of his pit of despair, says more than you can ever imagine.

For me, it's what is meant by the saying "Behind every successful man is a strong woman." And I believe it's the reason why a man never says he can do without a woman. We know that on any given day, the bottom might drop out of the normally full world we've been swimming around in, and often, it's you we turn to to plug that hole.

Integrating yourself into your guy's life really means just being there. And I don't mean you should carry him. I'm not suggesting you meet a guy and the next day you should put money in his pocket, or give him the keys to your car because he pawned his.

The man you support will be proven, a man who equally supports you. But not just in bad times. Being a constant part of your guy's life will also mean there will be times when great things happen, be it that promotion he's always wanted, graduation from school, the start of his own business, whatever. You being there with him for these moments—sharing in his success or helping him endure failure or loss—will let him know how much you truly care for him, which will, in turn, inform him of how invaluable you are to him now, and possibly for the rest of his life.

CHAPTER TEN

*And After All That, What to Do If
He Still Has Not Proposed*

Okay, so if after months of hanging out, going to the movies, grocery shopping, spending the night, talking on the phone, sending him text messages, and giving him great sex he still hasn't proposed, or doesn't even seem to be warming to the idea, something might be wrong, you're thinking. I'm sorry to say that you're probably right. What you must do now is appreciate that fact, respect that fact. Don't second-guess your feelings, and don't let your girlfriends talk you out of the fact that he might be trying to make you into a "bridge woman."

A woman never has to wonder if a man wants to marry her

You've been dating a guy for the last seven years. You're getting sick of waiting, of watching all your friends walk down the aisle, and you tell yourself all he needs is a firm shove in the back. And with the convincing of your friends, you give it to him. You give him The Ultimatum.

Let me say this—that's something a woman should never do. Never, never, never do! Because if you feel the need to do it, you've already answered whatever question or questions you have about this guy. The number one being—is he the guy you want to marry? And the answer is no.

After giving that man an ultimatum, one that generally sounds like this — "Either you marry me by [fill in the date] or I'm breaking up with you" — one of two things will happen. Either he will allow you to break up with him because, as he's shown you for the last seven years, he's never wanted marriage, or he'll give in and do exactly as you ask and marry you.

With the second result, you'll probably believe that you've won. That you got the man you always wanted. But he won't feel that way. He will feel that he was pressured into a situation, one that he never really wanted to begin with.

And when any little thing goes wrong, whenever he has the slightest doubt about whether he should be with you, or whether he loves you, he'll resent you and scold himself for crumbling under the pressure you placed on him.

So you should never give a man an ultimatum, and you should never feel you have to.

Why?

Because you'll never have to guess if a man wants to marry you. Just like you'll never have to guess if men are interested.

We walk right up to you on the street, try to get to know you and get your phone number. After that, we'll call you like crazy, take you out, spend money on you and try to cover as many bases as possible in a short period of time. Sure, we might also be trying to get sex from you, or that might even be the primary goal, but at least you don't have to wonder whether or not we are interested.

The same goes for marriage. If a man truly loves you, if he truly wants to marry you, he's often too gung ho about it.

Consider the guy on all the TV soap operas who, after only two months of dating, invites his girlfriend out to dinner to surprise her with a ring. All the while that ring is burning in his pocket, we the TV viewers are urging him, "Don't give her the ring. She's gonna say no!" But he does it anyway, because he's so excited about marrying this woman.

And what happens? Of course, she rejects him in front of the entire restaurant, and makes him look like a fool.

But those are the lengths to which we're willing to go.

I mean, haven't you seen those sappy, dopey proposals that are made public, where the guy asks for his girl's hand in marriage on the huge screen at the nationally televised baseball game. Or where a guy purchases the billboard space for his proposal over the most congested street in the city, the street he knows his girlfriend drives by every morning and night.

Wouldn't you prefer a guy who is that excited about marrying you to a guy you have to damn near threaten?

The sad thing is, after dealing with him all those years, you might not even believe that a man can look forward to marriage with that much enthusiasm. We can and we do.

Knowing if he has other women

I sat with a female friend of mine the other day. We discussed the new relationship she just started. She said she was tired of dating guys just to date. She had been married once before, and was looking forward to being married again, so she wasn't interested in a relationship that didn't have a good chance of heading in that direction. The cool thing was, she told the new guy that on the second or third date.

He was taken aback a bit. She told me he said a woman had never brought it to him like that before.

"Good for you!" I said.

I hadn't even finished this book yet, but she had already implemented step 2.

She wanted my opinion as to whether he was on the up-and-up with her. I asked for a little more information. She told me they had gone out Friday, she spent the night at his house, and left the next morning. Then she said he had not called her since. It was now Monday evening.

"The guy is playing games," I told her.

She went into defense mode for her new man.

My friend let me know that in early conversations with him, he informed her that he was a very busy guy, that he was trying to become more successful, and that he would not be calling her every day, so she shouldn't expect that.

It often shocks me how you ladies can't detect when a steaming pile of fresh puppy crap has been dumped right at your feet.

Very early on this man established the rules, gave them to the woman—my friend—and demanded that she abide by those rules. And she did just that.

Yes, they went out Friday night. Yes, that night they had sex. And no, he was not required to call her for three days, or see her for another week, because he told her he was busy. Wow.

Game. Nothing but game.

"But what if he *is* really busy?" my friend asked me.

No one is really so busy that he can't make a thirty-second call and say, "Hey, babe. I'm really busy, but just wanted to give you a ring and let you know I'm thinking about you."

That was two sentences that took fifteen seconds, five if you don't count ring time.

Or how about sending a text message?

With all the typing this successful guy probably does during his workday, he can't type a line or two to the woman he had just slept with over the weekend? Give me a freakin' break!

Know this much. If a guy likes you, but is really busy, when he does have a break or time off, he's going to spend that time with you. On the way from his second job to his third, he will stop by your house for a kiss and a hug if he really likes you.

So don't fall for the "I'm really busy" thing. It's just not the case.

Men want to share time with someone else as much as you do. And after a certain age, around that mid-thirty mark I keep talking about, men don't even like to sleep alone. That's not to say that he has a different woman in his bed every night, but if you're in a relationship with a guy and he can't contact you at least once a day, then there are other things going on.

I won't run down an entire list of ways to know if your guy is seeing other women. It's been done so many times that you probably know the signs better than you know your ABCs. What I will say is this, let your gut decide. Let your intuition determine whether that man is doing right by you.

It really is as simple as that.

If you think there's something going on and you approach him with it, and he says there isn't, like you know he's going to say, don't listen to words. Actions speak much louder, right?

I happen to be part of a family that doesn't use the "I love you" thing much. We don't say it a lot. I think I may have said it to my mother like three times in my life, and that goes the same for her. But never, ever, would I question the love that each one of my family members has for me, solely because they prove it in their actions.

A man can devise any argument to make you seem as though you're being irrational. It's what we do. Trust me, we have decades of experience dealing with irrational woman, making you see things our way, even when you're right and we're more wrong than wrong can ever be.

Bottom line, if he has you questioning whether he's devoted, then simply because you have to consider asking the question, by default he's not. If he has you thinking that he's cheating, it's not as though he even has to actually be out there with other women; he can just be neglecting you, which means he is indeed cheating you. He's cheating you of your time, and of the security, the love, and all the great things that you could have with another man who truly respects you.

Sticking to your guns, and knowing when to walk away

I know, ending a relationship, especially a long one, is very hard to do. But if you know, if you are sure that you want marriage, and every indication that he has given you proves he does not, then why stay with him? That is, unless you intend to alter your wants to meet his needs, which I recommend you not do, just like I recommend that you not give a man an ultimatum.

Obviously, the key is to find a man who wants what you want. Yes, it seems to be the hardest thing in the world to do, especially if you're single right now, which means that your entire life you have not been able to find him.

I know, when I put it that way, it makes the situation sound even that much more desperate. But one thing I know is that it is not worth staying in a relationship that you know is not fulfilling, that is not as loving as you want it to be, just to say that you are in one. If you've given that man all you have to give, if you let him know that you really want to marry him, love him, care for him, be faithful to him, and have him do the same for you, and he's not responding, then you have to walk away.

There is no conversation that needs to be had, because, as I told you before, we can talk you into anything. And we will.

"Come on, baby. Just give me a little more time," we'll say. And that little more time will stretch into three more years. Place that on top of the seven you just gave him, and you've devoted a decade of your life to a man who was just taking up space.

You're telling yourself that you've been with him that long, which means the relationship wasn't really that bad.

Well if "not really that bad" is all you're looking for, then there's no need to complain. You really didn't even have to pick up this book, because you're right where you want to be, in a relationship that will just do, a relationship that really does nothing more than keep you from being single.

And that is what we all fear, right? Growing old and being alone.

But think about all the other women who feared that and stuck with the guys they were with, and just remained life partners. Not that there is anything wrong with that. But a man who's been with you that long and does not marry you has a reason. More often than not, it's because he doesn't want to lock himself down, for fear of what he really wants all of a sudden popping up.

But let's say another five years goes by and he does eventually realize that his total-package woman will never show, and so he decides to marry you. Is that really what you want? Someone to settle for you?

And don't act as though you won't know it. The man has been with you for ten or fifteen years, and now, at the age of fifty-one, he decides to make you his bride. At best, you're a consolation prize. At worst, for the rest of your life you'll be married to a man who was never really that enthused about being with you in the first place.

You don't want that.

What you want is a man who will introduce himself to you, tell you that he's interested, and ask to take you out. You want a man who, after telling him you're looking for a relationship that could lead to marriage, will say, "I'm looking for the same thing." And you want him to mean it.

You want a man to know that you're a wonderful woman, that many other men would be honored and privileged to be given the time that you are giving him, and you want that man to show you that he feels that way.

You want that man to invite you into his life, to spend time getting to know you, to allow you to meet his friends and family, and to want to meet yours.

That man will be devoted to getting to know you, and only you, on a more personal level. With each day and week and month that passes, he'll give you more reason to believe that he could be the man you want to spend the rest of your life with.

With this man, you won't have to worry about constantly reminding him that you want this to lead to marriage, because even though the conversation isn't brought up every other day, his actions prove that he's moving with that goal in mind.

This man will tell you how he feels, but more important, he'll show you. He'll know what you enjoy, what you love, because you told him, and he will do those things with you.

You will not question his fidelity to you, because he will give you no reason to.

He will be there when you need him, give you what you ask for, within reason, and tell you no when you know you're being a little ridiculous.

He will honor, respect, and love you. He will talk about the future with you, and you'll be included not only in that conversation but also in that future.

And then one day, after a year or two or three, when you least expect it, though you always knew it was a possibility, he'll present a ring to you and ask you to marry him. There will be no doubt in your mind, no question as to whether or not things will work out between the two of you.

You'll simply say yes, because your heart will give you no other choice.

That is what you want, and you should not be willing to accept less.

Men fear marriage just like children fear ghosts, because of scary stories that have been told to us, and for reasons we know may not be true but our imaginations have made a reality. But just like those kids, who grew up and realized that ghosts aren't real, or told themselves that even if they are, they will just have to be accepted, men eventually do the same thing. We grow up, mature, and accept whatever fear we may have had regarding marriage. We test the stories for validity, question ourselves about what we believe and what we can deal with, because we realize that we want what you ladies have always wanted. We want companionship, unconditional love, and lifelong devotion. It just takes a moment—a little longer for some of us than for others—but bear with us. Eventually we come around, we become brave, we know what we want, and, in turn, we make you know by telling you point-blank, "I love you and I want you to be my wife. Will you marry me?"

But if the man you're dealing with or the man you want doesn't come around when you need him to, and then walks away because maybe he has not grown up yet, maybe he still fears marriage. (And if that's the case, he's no more good to you than a child who still fears ghosts.)

CHAPTER ELEVEN

Finally . . . Why Men Really Fear Marriage

Every night I crawl into bed, pull the blankets up to my chest, and just lie there, staring up at the ceiling. This is the part of my day, the part of my life, that I believe I like the least—going to bed by myself. I'm not quite sure why, but this is the time when I'm most reminded that I'm alone, that I have not done what I should've done some time ago—shake whatever fears I have and get married. Not because I'm supposed to, or because at forty years old I believe my time is running out. I should've done that, still should do that, because it's what I want. It's what most men want, but for those who have not yet done it, I've realized that the only reason is the fact that we are simply frightened to death.

An old friend once told me, "You just step off and fall, and have faith that everything will be fine."

The thought of a man plummeting, his arms flapping, legs flailing, body falling perilously, is beyond scary. That man has no control. It's not solely up to him if his marriage works. He could be as cooperative and caring as he could possibly be, but if his other half decides she no longer wants marriage, or wants to make it a living hell for him, then that's what it will be.

Being a man of forty, I obviously have control issues. I've steered my own boat since I left the nest at eighteen. Am I ready to give that up? Am I willing? I say that I am, but my actions prove otherwise.

This is the same for so many men out there. So don't believe that we don't want you. We do. Don't believe that we don't love you. We absolutely adore you, and we long to have you by our sides.

We just don't know if we want you there for the rest of our lives. And we don't know whether we want to deal with whatever problems, no matter how small, may arise because of our marriage to you. And we don't know if we want the responsibility of being accountable, or the burden of your children, or the guilt of desiring other women when we know we should be faithful only to you.

That's the real reason why men fear marriage. Because we are cowards when it comes to not knowing what the future may hold. But this is not natural behavior for us. We won't jump, startled like a cat, if you sneak up and clap your hands behind our backs. We have reason for our fear and trepidation. All the things you have just read about make us pause, make us fast-forward however far into the future and envision ourselves next to you. We might be happier than we've ever been. But we might also be so miserable that we'd ask ourselves, why did we give up what we had just to experience pain and anger and sadness with you?

So that's what men consider, and that's what freezes us. As single men, we know what we have, and for the most part, we are comfortable with it. We have a place to live, a car to drive, a job that makes us money, but, most of all, we have our freedom.

If we like you, we'll continue seeing you. If we think we don't, we'll move on to the next one, or two or three. Doing that, we won't gain anything. We won't grow close enough to you that we'd even consider spending the rest of our lives with you. But doing it this way, we also won't lose anything.

So we will continue to go to bed by ourselves at night. And as we reach over and click off the bedside lamp, we will tell ourselves it is worth it, at least for now. Because even though we are lonely, we take comfort in knowing that tomorrow night we will still be in control of our lonely lives.

Printed in the United States
By Bookmasters